TAOISM UNDER THE T'ANG

T. H. BARRETT

TAOISM
UNDER THE
T'ANG

RELIGION & EMPIRE
DURING THE GOLDEN AGE
OF CHINESE HISTORY

wellsweep

ILLUSTRATIONS
Illustrations within the book on pages 7 , 53 & 92 are sages and immortals taken from the *Li-tai shen-hsien t'ung-chien*. Cover jacket artwork is based on the illustration to a poem by Ku K'uang in Huang Feng-chih ed. *Ch'i-yen T'ang-shih hua-p'u*.

First published in 1996 by
The Wellsweep Press
1 Grove End House
150 Highgate Road
London NW5 1PD

ISBN 0 948454 98 9

BRITISH LIBRARY CATALOGUING-IN-PUBLICATION DATA
A catalogue record for this book is available from the British Library.

Designed and typeset by *Wellsweep*

PREFACE

Students of mediaeval Chinese history in the West will be well aware that though the *Cambridge History of China* has already devoted a volume to the political fortunes of the T'ang dynasty, the series still lacks a second volume on other aspects of the T'ang experience, despite the completion of several fine chapters for this project second part some time ago. This has led to the appearance already of two monographs based on the unpublished chapters, both from Cambridge University Press, namely *Buddhism under the T'ang* by my doctoral supervisor, Stanley Weinstein, and *Statesmen and Scholars*, by my undergraduate supervisor, David McMullen. When I was first asked about fifteen years ago by Denis Twitchett to sketch out a companion chapter on Taoism under the T'ang to go with the draft studies on which these monographs were based, it was understood in view of the dearth of publications available in the field of Taoist studies at that time that my own efforts would not aim at the same standard of comprehensive coverage as that achieved by my teachers. As a result, the outline history I eventually produced appeared at first a rather unlikely prospect for independent publication, and was merely circulated to the very limited number of persons who expressed interest in my work.

They, in turn, it seems, have been asked by their friends for further copies, as over the past decade or so T'ang Taoism has gradually become a more popular area for research, with the result that references to my draft have become increasingly common, and have even turned up in reading lists and bibliographic surveys. Yet since the distribution of copies has so far been a purely private matter, not everyone has had a chance to gain access to this material, and many scholars directly involved in research into T'ang religion have been obliged in the absence of the second *Cambridge History of China* volume on the T'ang to publish their own work without consulting my findings, thus

5

duplicating research efforts. In late 1994 I had the opportunity to discuss this situation with Professor Twitchett, who agreed that matters had developed so as to merit the separate publication of this study, in order that my work, already drawn on by a number of researchers, might be open to wider scrutiny. My own feeling on reading through what I wrote in its original form was that despite the appearance of a fair number of specialised publications touching on T'ang Taoism during the intervening years, as a broad narrative, in particular of the involvement of the ruling house in Taoist religion throughout the life of the dynasty, my brief outline still had a certain part to play, and indeed that though I might wish now to modify a few passages, what I had written was not itself seriously misleading or inaccurate.

In this judgement, of course, I may have been deceiving myself, though if so I hope that the normal process of reviewing will quickly set me straight. I thought it better in any case that this study should be placed in the public domain in the form in which it has already given some guidance to researchers, rather than that the eventual appearance solely of a slightly expanded and corrected version should mislead later scholars as to the form in which it has been circulated so far. Naturally, I have not striven to preserve all the blemishes in the original, but have taken the opportunity to remove some typographical and other minor errors, thanks to the good offices of Professor Twitchett and of Ralph Meyer of Princeton University; they, however, should certainly not be held responsible for any such errors that may remain.

During the original drafting of this work I was assisted by a number of colleagues in locating materials: Stanley Weinstein, for example, put me on to the doctoral work of Charles Benn at an early stage, thus saving me a great deal of work with primary sources at a particularly complex point in the story. It has given me great pleasure to see that Dr Benn has been able to pursue and bring to publication further work in this field; though our paths have never crossed, he may like to know that the thought that my work was not entirely without precedent made the going a great deal easier. The librarians at Cambridge responsible for the Chinese and Japanese collections at the time when I undertook this work were Helen Spillett and Ceci Whitford; to them and especially to the first honorary Curator of the Chinese collection, Professor Piet van der Loon, I owe a debt extending well beyond any specific help they gave me at the time. Dr Helen Dunstan, now of MIT, and Dr Helen Soo, now a colleague in my own department in London, were most helpful in securing materials from Japan and Hong Kong respectively. John Lagerwey was kind enough to provide some early criticism of my efforts, while Nathan Sivin gave me valuable support at an even earlier stage of my first explorations of Taoist studies. To all who helped me then I am relieved at last to be able to show slim recompense for their generosity, though I am sorry if this is not the stout monograph that they may have been hoping for at the time.

That my work should appear at this point is due to the generosity and forbearance of a number of other sources of support. Financial support has come from the Spalding Trust, and also from the Publications Committee of the School of Oriental and African Studies; I am much indebted to both for underwriting a somewhat unusual publishing project of this type. My student Duncan Begg volunteered to carry out the necessary xeroxing; I hope that he and his classmates find the results worthwhile. John Cayley, despite many other demands on his time, agreed to take on the task of publication itself — a decision which has made matters much easier for me, though not for him. Above all, I am grateful to Denis Twitchett for his efforts on my behalf throughout. This is by no means the first publication under my name which has derived from work he initially suggested to me in earlier years, but since I have enjoyed every task he has ever set me, perhaps it will not be the last.

T. H. Barrett
Shepreth
March 1995

Contents

ABBREVIATIONS

The abbreviations (where not otherwise noted) and editions used are those specified in Denis Twitchett, ed., *Cambridge History of China (CHC)*, volume 3 (Cambridge, 1979), pp. xiv–xv, or in the draft chapter by Stanley Weinstein (sometimes mentioned below), now published as *Buddhism under the T'ang* (Cambridge, 1987), p. 151.

CKFL	*Chi ku-chien Fo Tao lun-heng*
CSHP	*Chin-shih hsu-pien*
CSTP	*Chin-shih ts'ui-pien*
CTS	*Chiu T'ang shu*
CTW	*Ch'üan T'ang-wen*
CYYY	*Kuo-li chung-yang yen-chiu yüan Li-shih yü-yen yen-chiu-so chi-k'an* (Academia Sinica)
FYCL	*Fa-yüan chu-lin*
HJAS	*Harvard Journal of Asian Studies*
HTS	*Hsin T'ang shu*
SPTK	Ssu-pu ts'ung-k'an edn.
TCTC	*Tzu-chih t'ung-chien*
TFYK	*Ts'e-fu yüan-kuei*
THY	*T'ang hui-yao*
TLT	*T'ang liu-tien*
TP	*T'oung pao*
TSCC	Ts'ung-shu chi-ch'eng edn.
TTCLC	*T'ang ta ch'ao-ling chi*
WYYH	*Wen-yüan ying-hua*

BACKGROUND & EARLY YEARS

Any account of Taoism under the T'ang must be prefaced by a frank admission of our present ignorance of many aspects of Taoist history. This is not due to a lack of sources; rather, it is the result of the lack of a tradition of Taoist historiography. The historical study of the Taoist religion is a twentieth-century phenomenon, and largely a phenomenon of the last few decades at that. Much work remains to be done, though some of the major phases of development have become tolerably clear, and it is at least possible to provide a sketch of the period prior to the T'ang dynasty itself.[1]

Most scholars of the Taoist religion today, whilst ready to acknowledge the great antiquity of many Taoist ideas and practices, trace the origins of an organized religion that eventually came to refer to itself as Taoism back no further than the turbulent second century AD. Of the many religious movements that flourished during the final years of the Han dynasty and the period of chaos that followed, one in particular proved able to mount a challenge to established authority strong enough to have enduring consequences. This was the organization known as the "Way of the five Pecks of Rice," Wu-tou-mi tao, or "Way of the Celestial Master," T'ien-shih tao, which had been

---

[1] For the development of Taoist studies up to 1980, see H. Maspero, trans. Frank A. Kierman, Jr., *Taoism and Chinese Religion* (Amherst, 1981), pp. vii–xxiii. The following survey is based on the literature reviewed there, especially that produced by the first two international conferences on Taoism, plus one more recent and very important publication: M. Strickmann, *Le Taoisme du Mao-shan: chronique d'une revelation* (Paris, 1981). In hesitating to ascribe the entire corpus of the Ling-pao scriptures to Ko Ch'ao-fu, however, I take account of the research of Kobayashi Masayoshi, viz. "Ryū-Sō ni okeru *Reibō-kyō* no keisei," *Tōyō bunka* 62 (March, 1982), pp. 99–138, and *"Reibō sekisho gohen shimmon* no shisō to seiritsu," *Tōhō shūkyō* 60 (Oct., 1982), pp. 23–47.

founded in Szechwan by Chang Tao-ling in the mid-second century. As a "fighting church" under his grandson Chang Lu it finally negotiated a settlement in AD 215 with the Wei successors to the Han dynasty which allowed it to continue its religious activities not only in Szechwan but also in those areas of north China under Wei control. Thus its priests, the *chi-chiu*, or "libationers," who had provided the leadership in its original parishes in Szechwan, found adherents now among the ruling clans of the Wei and Chin dynasties.

When the latter dynasty was driven out of North China in the second decades of the fourth century its refugee elite took their religion with them to the region south of the Yangtze which the dynasty had earlier won from the state of Wu. In this area different religious traditions had persisted, including a wealth of occult lore dating back in all probability to Han times. At first the local aristocracy was prepared to accept the priests who had come with the refugees from the north, but by the seventh decade of the fourth century southern noble families who found their political position usurped by the northerners were ready to receive a completely new religious message, albeit one which owed much to the Way of the Celestial Master.

For though this new dispensation set itself up as superior to the Way of the Celestial Master in just the same fashion as Chang Tao-ling's teaching declared itself superior to the many local cults which flourished throughout China, it did not manifest the implacable opposition to the old order which distinguished Chang's followers. Rather, in a way which suited well the political situation of the recipients of the message, the deities invoked by the libationers were revealed as ranking below those of a realm of Supreme Purity, Shang-ch'ing. The source of these revelations was the visionary Yang Hsi (b. 330); as a spiritual intermediary replacing the libationers he catered to the needs of the southern aristocrat Hsü Mi (303–73) and his family. Hsü Mi was presented with teachings in Yang's powerful calligraphy which were just what he wanted: the old occult lore of the South and the new beliefs from the north blended together and developed into a fresh synthesis of religious practice and doctrine suitable for a court official, especially one who lacked the right friends in high places and so felt a need for impressive connections in the unseen world.

The reception of these new Shang-ch'ing scriptures, primarily associated with Hsü's retreat at Mao-shan near the Chin capital, amongst southern society was evidently enthusiastic. Not only were the scriptures themselves highly sought after and much imitated; the whole episode of their revelation appears to have inspired Ko Ch'ao-fu (whose wife was of the Hsü clan) and perhaps some others at a slightly later date during the final decade of the fourth century, to produce another entire corpus of sacred literature. These scriptures, the Ling-pao canon, similarly display both continuity with earlier religious belief and also new features — in this instance elements derived from Buddhism provided a further novelty. During the fifth century we see the emergence of distinguished religious leaders in the south, all from old southern families, who took up this heritage and ordered it into a single hierarchy of beliefs, starting with the *San-huang wen*, ancient texts which represented the religion of the south prior to the arrival of the Chin refugees, and ascending to the Ling-pao and Shang-ch'ing revelations.

Which of these two latter traditions was seen as the higher truth obviously depended on the allegiance of the particular leader in question, although the Taoists of Mao-shan appear to have eventually achieved the position of paramount school. At all events the different scriptural traditions seem at this stage to have been taken to constitute one higher, Chinese religion, whose different schools were ranged against the various teachings of the Buddhists. The place of the Way of the Celestial Master in this scheme was somewhat problematic; its libationers may have ministered to the spiritual needs of aristocrats, but they also had connections with the very different world of popular religion. Not only did their struggle with the adherents of popular local cults occasionally work to the corruption of their own status as the original proponents of a higher religion; intrinsic to that religion itself, it would seem, were orgiastic elements highly disturbing to aristocratic sensibilities.

Thus in north China also, under the T'o-pa Wei dynasty, we find a reformed version of Taoism established by revelation which sought to purify the Way of the Celestial Master as it was practised in that area. Here the agent of this revelation, which took place on Mount Sung in 415 and 423, was a Chinese from a respected family, K'ou Ch'ien-chih, and its chief promoter was another Chinese, Ts'ui Hao (381–450), a minister at the non-Chinese court. But in the harsher political climate of North China spiritual authority meant little without its direct conversion into temporal power, so here the members of the dispossessed elite lost little time in bringing the new dispensation to the attention of the T'o-pa ruler T'ai-wu (r. 424–52). K'ou's message was a welcome one to both minister and monarch. His revelations had the authority of the deified Lao-tzu, who since the late Han had represented an alternative type of sagehood to that of Confucius, and in whose name (or that of his emissary, Li Hung) many messianic insurrections had occurred. But here the sage communicated a strong desire to see good order established, with the T'o-pa emperor cast in the role of Taoist ruler. That the emperor should accept the reformation of religious life enjoined by a Chinese sage further suited Ts'ui's desire to sinify the Wei regime.

All went well from 425 onwards, to the point where Ts'ui felt in a position to call for a purge not only of the heterodox cults which had been the traditional target of the Way of the Celestial Master but also of the non-Chinese religion of Buddhism. The persecution of Buddhism which took place in 446 by no means established reformed Taoism as the uncontestable religion of the north; within less than a decade all three participants in this experiment were dead, and there is little to show that K'ou's movement, deprived of state support, was able to maintain its position independently. What is clear, however, is that by the late fifth century Taoism in both north and south China had developed to the point where it had achieved, despite somewhat disparate origins, a certain self-awareness as the Chinese alternative to Buddhism.

Within another century a new level of cohesion was achieved with the introduction of the sophisticated southern Taoism of the Mao-shan school and its analogues into north China. This process of northward diffusion may have been stimulated by measures taken to restrict Taoism in the first half of the sixth century under the southern Liang dynasty. At all events by the time that the emperor Chou Wu-ti of the Northern Chou (r. 560–78) came to the throne, he had before him not only ample precedents for the political use of Taoism but also a religion which could measure up in both its institutional and doctrinal aspects to any of its rivals.

True, Buddhism had arrived in China as a religion possessing a great wealth of scriptures which set forth doctrines from the warmly pietistic to the subtly philosophical. It also possessed great institutional strengths unknown in China before; a celibate clergy which renounced all prospect of secular involvements for a lifetime's dedication to their religion, and a conception of the religious value of charitable donations that rapidly led to wealthy monastic endowments which made clerical religious life possible. But although the Taoists were never able to match the concentrated economic strength of the Buddhist community they did benefit from these Buddhist notions of charity and of religious life, which were in themselves by no means alien to native Chinese concepts of religious merit, so that they, too, acquired endowed institutions inhabited by full-time and even celibate clergy.

Yet Taoism could (and does today) survive perfectly well without monasteries — certainly far more easily than the Buddhists, who were always vulnerable to governments envious of their riches. The distinction between a full-time and a self-supporting clergy, and even the distinction between a celibate and a married clergy, was by no means always a clear-cut one. Taoists priests were not called upon to renounce the world with quite the comprehensive finality demanded of Buddhist monks. Hence although we use the term "Taoist church" to refer to the Taoist priesthood and its adherents, this is simply a concise and convenient expedient employed to describe a rather loose collectivity which may not be thought of as in any way analogous to the Christian church or even the Buddhist community in China. Though it was doubtless in the interests of the government to operate clear and unambiguous definitions of the boundaries of the Taoist clergy, and perhaps even to impose upon the Taoists a pattern of spiritual life similar to that of the Buddhists, in reality such definitions could only have been somewhat arbitrary.

For the Taoists were not preaching any new religious message about the human condition but offering their expertise in dealing with the world of the supernatural. Thus they could live as individuals (or family men) from the fees prescribed for the transmission of sacred texts and the like. The libationers of the Way of the Celestial Master, for example, seem to have lived among their parishioners as members of the community removed from ordinary life only by their superior occult knowledge rather than any renunciation of secular ties; their leadership appears to have remained hereditary, even if the claims of an unbroken family succession from Chang Tao-ling to the present day are somewhat suspect.

This close relationship with local society made it possible for individual Taoist leaders to exploit the messianic tradition within Taoism so as to instigate mass uprisings against authori-

ties, though when Buddhist propagandists pointed to this unfortunate propensity of their rivals for fomenting rebellion they
conveniently ignored the fact that messianic beliefs associated
with their own faith had by the late sixth century also produced
popular insurrections. In so far as support for religion allowed
Chinese rulers to exercise a measure of control over elements of
society whose loyalty to them might be dubious there were
equally good reasons for extending their patronage to both
Taoists and Buddhists.

Where Taoism was clearly at an advantage in its relations with
the Chinese state was in its Chineseness. While Buddhism, for
all its accommodation to Chinese conditions, remained unmis-
takably a universal religion, Taoism was from the beginning to
end a natural outgrowth of native ways of thought and action.
The notion of individual responsibility expressed in the
Buddhist idea of karma contrasts in Taoist texts with the concern shown for the well-being of deceased ancestors and the
family as a whole. The grandiose Indian concepts of time and
space, of cosmic cycles of time and of innumerable
world-systems, were among the elements absorbed by Taoism in
the course of its development, but became no more than exten-
sions of a basically Chinese awareness of the physical world, and
particularly of the Chinese land itself, with its sacred peaks and
rivers.

At the same time Taoism could go far beyond the conceptions
of heaven, earth and man enshrined in the texts of
Confucianism. In particular it allowed the emperor, the Son of
Heaven, to play his part as intermediary between heaven and
man against a far more impressive background than that envis-
aged in the system of imperial Confucian ideology evolved under the Han dynasty. In this way it could provide an attractive
means to self-aggrandizement to rulers whose position among
the powerful competing clans of sixth (and seventh) century
north China was often decidedly insecure. Thus the decision of

emperor Wu of the Northern Chou to give his support to the Taoists and persecute Buddhism may be seen as a measure based on sound political judgement rather than religious bias, and as but one of his measures designed to create a strong, unified state capable of achieving the conquest of the whole of China.

The Northern Chou emperor's religious policy has presented a rather confusing picture to later historians, who have sometimes portrayed him as an enemy of all religions; certainly he was only interested in promoting religion if it was of direct advantage to himself.[2] Thus after it emerged in debate between Taoists and Buddhists during the earlier part of his reign that the Way of the Celestial Master was vulnerable to Buddhist criticism of its association with sedition and immorality, we find no reference at all to its priesthood and rituals in the imperially-sponsored encyclopaedia of Taoism, the *Wu-shang pi-yao*. Rather, this compilation draws upon the Taoism of the aristocratic schools of southern China, supplemented by rituals written by (or at the behest of) the emperor himself. These latter rituals, however, manifest a number of elements clearly drawn from the traditions of the Way of the Celestial Master and from Buddhism itself. In other words, the emperor seems to have conceived of a scheme to absorb all the religious practice of his day into a Taoist church firmly under his own control.

But this bold and imaginative policy did not survive the emperor's death in 578, and when the Sui dynasty finally realised his dream of reunifying the whole of China they seem to have been

---

[2] The interpretation of Northern Chou Taoism given here is drawn in large part from J. Lagerwey, *Wu-shang pi-yao: somme Taoiste du VIe siècle* (Paris, 1981). The views of Kubo Noritada on this period are somewhat different; see his *Chūgoku shūkyō ni okeru juyō, hen'yō, gyōyō* (Tokyo, 1979), pp. 26–68. Lagerwey would appear to be supported by Sunayama Minoru, "Ubun Yū no *Dōkyō Jikka jo* ni tsuite," *Bukkyō shigaku kenkyū* 21:1 (June, 1978), pp. 46–75.

more concerned to use the existing religious situation in their efforts to weld together their new empire rather than to impose upon it a single form of religion of their own devising. As is well known, the ideological complexion of the Sui regime was strongly tinged with Buddhism, even if not to the total exclusion of Taoism. For it was Buddhism which in actual fact spanned the cultural and social divisions which had arisen in the long period of disunity; the realization of Taoism's ideological potential lay as yet in the future.

Nor, for all the brevity of the Sui success, did it lie in the immediate future. The spectacular collapse of their empire created a chaos in which the implementation of carefully constructed policies towards religion was quite out of the question. This is not to deny that their successors, the T'ang, were from the first to last closely involved in Taoism. This short monograph would be even shorter were it not for the ever increasing number of scholars who have chosen to comment on the relationship between Taoism and the T'ang ruling house, and until we know much more about the development of Taoism as a whole any treatment of T'ang Taoism must perforce concentrate on that relationship.[3] For whatever the precedents under earlier dynasties, the T'ang must be recognized as marking the high tide of Taoist influence upon Chinese political life. The

[3] Two substantial studies on this topic have been produced in Chinese: Fang Yung-hsien, "T'ang-tai huang-shih yü tao-chiao," M.A. thesis University of Hong Kong, 1966, the first half of which was published in five parts in *Ching feng* 18 (Sept. 1968), pp. 28–42; 19 (Dec. 1968), pp. 66–78; 21 (June 1969), pp. 67–89; 22 (Sept. 1969), pp. 80–89; 23 (Dec. 1969), pp. 81–100; and Sun K'o-k'uan, "T'ang-tai tao-chiao yü cheng-chih," in *Han-yüan tao-lun* (Taipei, 1977), pp. 59–165. For the first century of the dynasty Charles David Benn, "Taoism as Ideology in the Reign of Emperor Hsüan-tsung (712–755)," Ph.D. Diss. University of Michigan, 1977, provides a good introductory chapter, besides a thorough treatment of the reign indicated. Several shorter studies have also appeared in Chinese and Japanese.

very name of the dynasty itself may well have been chosen for its Taoist overtones.[4]

The reason most often cited for the prominence of Taoism at the T'ang court, however, seems at first sight remarkably trivial. The T'ang emperors bore the surname Li; this was the surname which Lao-tzu was said to have borne. Deeming themselves to be descendants of the sage, the T'ang emperors supported Taoism on family grounds. But family grounds were no trivial matter to the T'ang ruling house: in actual fact they were descended from a grouping of aristocrats which was in all likelihood far from purely Chinese and which consequently was ranked somewhat below the top of Chinese society in the north. Thus the claim of descent from an ancient Chinese sage, asserted in the most grandiose manner possible through their patronage of Taoism, represented a very necessary way of enhancing family prestige.

Curiously enough, at the start of the seventh century the Li surname probably had much more significance for the lower levels of society than for the aristocracy. As noted above, both Lao-tzu and the associated figure of Li Hung were looked to as potential saviours who might intervene in history at any moment. The "myth of the Li messiah" cannot be discounted as a factor in the successful foundation of the T'ang, though we might do well to remember that the deliberate circulation of prophecies that a ruler named Li would succeed the Sui was actually started by another contender for power who bore that name.[5] It would have been mildly surprising had matters been otherwise; the T'ang were aristocratic leaders, not rabble-rousers, and were inherently more likely to be in sympathy with the sophisticated southern schools of Taoism now established in the north, in

[4] See note 41 of Yoshioka Yoshitoyo, "Jihaku to Jiboku ni tsuite," in *Satō hakase koki kinen Bukkyō shisō ronsō* (Tokyo, 1972), pp. 609–27; and cf. Strickmann, p. 214 and p. 273, note 39.
[5] See the *The Cambridge History of China*, vol. 3, p. 154.

which "Li messiah" had been transmuted into a figure of much less revolutionary political significance.

Quite possibly the T'ang founders were able to exploit dissatisfaction with the Sui bias towards Buddhism amongst adherents to this more respectable form of Taoism. But here, too, it is necessary to be cautious. Although some of the men who helped found the T'ang dynasty do seem to have been drawn from among the Taoist clergy, other contenders for power, not all bearing the Li surname, were just as successful in attracting support form the same quarter.[6] So, also, the tales of theophanies accompanying the T'ang rise to power undoubtedly reflect a measure of Taoist support for their cause. But we should bear in mind that the clear link between Taoism and the imperial line drawn in narratives of these events as they appear in later sources, composed when that link was an undoubted political reality, is quite absent in the earliest reports.

Rather than seeking reasons for the T'ang patronage of Taoism solely in the immediate circumstances of the establishment of the dynasty, then, a knowledge of the earlier background of Northern Wei and Northern Chou state support for Taoism suggests that it evolved as a result of deeper causes. Far from being a mere aberration stemming from an adventitious coincidence of nomenclature, T'ang support for Taoism may be seen as a logical answer to the ideological and cultural problems facing a dynasty of northern origins grappling with the problems of exerting its control over an empire far larger than any that had been maintained in China for several centuries.

Even the very first reference to any act of Taoist worship on the part of the T'ang founder, Li Yüan, casual though it may be,

[6] For Taoism and the founding of the T'ang, see Miyakawa Hisayuki, *Rikuchōshi kenkyū — shūkyō hen* (Kyoto, 1964), pp. 176–187. For an example of Taoist support for a rival contender for power, see *TCTC* 187, p. 5850.

illustrates very well the potential that Taoism possessed for uniting the ethnically disparate inhabitants of north China in devotion to a purely Chinese cult. In 617, even before Li Yüan had mounted an open challenge to the Sui, he had opened negotiations with the Eastern Turks. After trading in horses the Turkish commander is said to have entered a temple dedicated to Lao-tzu, followed by the future emperor; the incident is only recorded because this order of precedence is said to have upset a Taoist priest present in Li Yüan's retinue.[7]

This awareness of the diplomatic value of the religion was to prove one of the most unusual features of state support for Taoism during Li Yüan's reign as T'ang Kao-tsu and during the reign of his successor T'ai-tsung. For in 624, and again perhaps in 643, missions were sent to the Korean kingdom of Koguryŏ, apparently at the latter's request, to propagate the Taoist religion there. The mission is said to have consisted of Taoist priests, who brought images of Taoist divinities and gave lectures on the *Tao-te ching*. Students from Koguryŏ also were allowed to come to China to study Taoism, just as their fellow-countrymen and others came to study Buddhism.[8] Against such a background the request of T'ai-tsung in 647 that the Buddhist pilgrim Hsüan-tsung should translate the *Tao-te ching* into Sanskrit for circulation in India appears much less bizarre than at first sight would seem to be the case, and scattered sources suggest that a similar scheme may have been put into effect to propagandize Tibet during the early eighth century, whilst Japan certainly made a similar request to that of Koguryŏ in 735.[9] Indeed the presence of a considerable number of

---

[7] See Miyazaki, p. 179, and for Turkish acceptance of Taoism cf. Bilgä Qaghan, who in 716 proposed building a capital in the Chinese style with both Buddhist and Taoist monasteries (*CTS* 194A, p. 5174).

[8] Kubo, pp. 189–192.

[9] For India and the *Tao-te ching* see P. Pelliot, "Autour d'une traduction sanscrite du *Tao-tö king*," *TP* 13 (1912), pp. 350–430; for Japan, *TFYK*

Taoist texts amongst the manuscripts of Tun-huang, a Buddhist center of long standing on the fringes of China proper, and the discovery of some Taoist charms and even indications of a Taoist monastery as far west as Karakhoja, indicate that the T'ang emperors were not necessarily misguided in hoping that the Taoist religion might expand beyond the homeland of Chinese civilization, though the net diplomatic benefits derived from their efforts appear to have been nil.[10]

Efforts to make use of Taoism in internal policy, on the other hand, cannot be said to have played a major part in the first two reigns. Early T'ang policy towards religion in general seems rather to mark a sharp break with the policies of the preceding dynasties. Both the Northern Chou and the Sui had supported Taoist institutions in the capital which acted as national centres of Taoist learning, though the latter dynasty had given an even greater measure of support to Buddhist institutions.[11] No such institutions of any sort were set up by the early T'ang rulers, and apart from a transitional period when a collective leadership of elderly and eminent Buddhists was accorded some sort of status, the early T'ang, unlike previous dynasties, also preferred to deal directly with religious communities rather than with intermediaries who were recognized spokesmen for or overseers of their fellow clergy at a national or regional level. Details of the way in which the government regulated the Taoist church at this time are hard to come by, but one incident which took place in 648 gives some indication of the type of measures which were in force at that date.

999:18b; for Tibet, P. Demiéville, in M. Soymié, ed., *Contributions aux études sur Touen-houang* (Genève-Paris, 1979), p. 6.

[10] See Ogasawara Senshū, "Seiiki shutsudo no jiryō monjo sairon," *Indogaku Bukkyōgaku kenkyū* 8:1 (Jan. 1960), pp. 105–9.

[11] Yamazaki Hiroshi, *Zui-Tō Bukkyōshi no kenkyū* (Kyoto, 1967), pp. 65–84.

A report in the Buddhist encyclopaedia *Fa-yüan chu-lin* states that in this year local authorities in Chi-chou (in present-day Kiangsi) found that the wife of a prisoner there possessed a copy of the *San-huang ching* which claimed that any woman possessing it would become an empress. Under interrogation she asserted that she had obtained it from a Taoist priest. The offending document was then rushed to the capital, where two Taoists from the Hsi-hua kuan were questioned about its subversive contents. They replied that the work had been written by a Taoist author of an earlier age but that this was an illegitimate copy of it; it was not something which they had produced themselves. The work was nonetheless proscribed. An official responsible for the statutes on the distribution of land pointed out that this scripture played a similar role for Taoists as ordination did for Buddhists in qualifying them for a grant of land; if it were destroyed the Taoists would lose these rights. The Taoists in the capital then asked that the *Tao-te ching* should be used in place of the *San-huang ching*. After this had been agreed all copies of the latter were collected and destroyed.[12]

Though this proscription does not seem to have had the desired effect of halting the transmission of this corpus of scripture, which reappears under its more normal title of *San-huang wen* at a later date, the incident has been used as evidence for the early existence in the T'ang of statutes granting particular land rights to the clergy; it has been suggested that these statutes may have come into force as early as 624.[13] Equally revealing is the use of the *San-huang wen* to determine membership of the Taoist clergy. For over two centuries prior to this time the Taoist Canon had been divided into three sections representing three different schools, of which that associated with the *San-huang wen* was deemed to be the least doctrinally profound. By the

12 *FYCL* 55, p. 708a–b, and cf. Ch'en Kuo-fu, *Tao-tsang yüan-liu k'ao* (Peking, 1963), pp. 77–8.
13 See Shigenoi Shizuka, *Tōdai Bukkyō shiron* (Kyoto, 1973), pp. 131–6.

seventh century more elaborate schemes of classification had developed, which included a grouping of texts associated with the *Tao-te ching*. It is highly unlikely that mere possession of the works mentioned in the *Fa-yüan chu-lin*'s account qualified one for membership in the clergy.

The reference would rather seem to be to the Taoist practice of doctrinal transmission whereby texts were only transmitted to believers through initiation rituals which included the taking of vows similar to the Buddhist monastic precepts; the hedging about of the *Tao-te ching* with such rituals had already attracted comment from outsiders by the mid-sixth century, and documents from the eighth century connected with such rituals are preserved among the Tun-huang manuscripts.[14] Though our present state of knowledge of the subject does not allow us to be sure how different groups of texts were graded by Taoists in the mid-seventh century, and though all such listings (as in the case of the tripartite division assigning a low value to the *San-huang wen*) were probably at least partly polemical in intent, one particular scheme which was to assume some importance by the end of the century not only places the *Tao-te ching* at a stage before the *San-huang wen* but also lists groups of texts relating to degrees of initiation (one of which clearly carries the clerical title *fa-shih*) at a level prior even to the *Tao-te ching*.[15] It would thus seem possible that even after 648 the government did not recognize as members of the clergy initiates who were so regarded by the Taoist church itself.

[14] Ch'en, *Tao-tsang yüan-liu k'ao*, p. 469; Ch'en Tsu-lung, "Tun-huang Tao ching hou chi hui lu," *Ta-lu tsa-chih* 25:10 (Dec., 1962), pp. 10–11; Lagerwey, *Wu-shang pi-yao*, pp. 125–29.

[15] This is the scheme given in the *Feng-tao k'o*, described below, for which see pp. 197–201 of the translation in Yoshioka Yoshitoyo, *Dōkyō to Bukkyō* III (Tokyo, 1976), pp. 161–219; Yoshioka's views on the origins of the text are given on pp. 77–159.

A further point of interest concerns the Taoists of the Hsi-hua kuan. Several of the Taoist manuscripts retrieved at Tun-huang were actually copied at monasteries in the capital, which suggests that such institutions acted as disseminators of Taoist literature to the provinces, and perhaps provides an explanation for the government's interrogation of the Taoist leaders; their characterization of the offending document as an illegitimate copy even hints that a centralization of the copying of Taoist texts had been encouraged precisely in order that it might be more easily susceptible to government control. One of the Taoists concerned in this case was a particularly prominent author of commentaries named Ch'eng Hsüan-ying, who had the previous year been involved in the translation of the *Tao-te ching* into Sanskrit; the prefatory remarks to a work of his interpreting the *Tao-te ching* have been recovered at Tun-huang, and a sub-commentary on the *Chuang-tzu* and his annotations to the *Tu-jen ching*, chief scripture of the Ling-pao school of Taoism, have also been preserved. From these, and from other references to his work, it is possible to discern that he belonged to a school of interpretation which borrowed a large number of concepts from Buddhism in its treatment of Taoist scripture.[16]

Such a trend in interpretation had in fact already become apparent long before the T'ang, and was in part no doubt a consequence of the formal debates between adherents of Buddhism, Taoism and Confucianism that had come to be held at intervals before various Chinese rulers. Though these degenerated in the latter half of the T'ang into mere exercises in debating skills, during the seventh century they were much more of a forum for

---

[16] On Ch'eng and his school, see Isabelle Robinet, *Les Commentaires du Tao To king jusqu'au VIIe siècle* (Paris, 1977), pp. 97–203, 228–260; and more recently Sunayama Minoru, "Dōkyō chūgen-ha hyōbi — Zui, sho Tō ni okeru Dōkyō no ichi keifu," *Shūkan Tōyōgaku* 43 (May, 1980), pp. 31–44, and "Sei Gen'ei no shisō ni tsuite," *Nihon Chūgoku gakkai hō* 32 (1980), pp. 125–139.

the clash of ideas. Since the Indian religion clearly possessed a much more refined system of philosophical terminology the Taoists not infrequently took the obvious step of appropriating their opponent's ideas and using (or attempting to use) them to their own ends.[17] In the first such debate to take place under the T'ang, in 624, representatives of all three traditions are said to have been vanquished by Lu Te-ming, who was familiar with the terminology of Buddhism and Taoism as well as being an outstanding Confucian scholar. The following year, however, Kao-tsu announced that Taoism should be ranked first, ahead of Confucianism, and that Buddhism should be ranked last, since it was a foreign religion.[18]

When this ranking of Taoism ahead of Buddhism was confirmed by T'ai-tsung in 637, the former religion was explicitly connected with the T'ang ruling house. Though there is no mention of this in 625, the following year saw the engraving of an inscription which states the connection unequivocally and reveals much besides concerning Taoist support for the T'ang in its earliest years. This inscription was made at the Lou-kuan, a Taoist monastery on Mount Chung-nan, south of Ch'ang-an, which had been since the fifth century a prime center of the religion in the north, well connected with whichever regime held power in the area.[19] The abbot in charge at the time of the fall of the Sui, Ch'i Hui, apparently threw in his lot with the T'ang as early as 617, providing supplies for the T'ang armies; he has even been suspected of having staged one of the theophanies which accompanied the T'ang rise to power. This support

---

[17] For a study of this practice throughout the T'ang, see Lo Hsiang-lin, "T'ang-tai san-chiao chiang-lun k'ao," in his *T'ang-tai wen-hua shih* (Taipei, 1955), pp. 159–176, and for an apparent instance of such appropriation as a result of these debates, Kamata Shigeo, *Chūgoku Bukkyō shisōshi kenkyū* (Tokyo, 1969), pp. 100–111.

[18] *CTS* 189, p. 4945; *CKFL* 2, p. 318a.

[19] For a brief history of this center see Ch'en, *Tao-tsang yüan-liu k'ao*, pp. 261–4.

was rewarded with grants of land in 619, and in 620 further benevolence was accompanied by an instruction that the name of the monastery should be changed to Tsung-sheng kuan, a move already designed to show that the T'ang leaders were placing themselves in the family line of the sage Lao-tzu. The inscription of 626 confirms this intent, and in its review of the history of the monastery incidentally demonstrates the cultural value attached to Taoism by describing the promotion of the religion at the expense of Buddhism in 446 as a move towards sinification.[20]

Relations between the early T'ang and the leaders of the southern Taoist tradition based at Mao-shan are less well-attested by contemporary documents. The preeminent figure of this movement at the time was a venerable figure named Wang Yüan-chih, who was reputedly aged one hundred and twenty-five at the time of his death in 635. Despite having received conspicuous honours from the Sui he is said to have predicted the T'ang rise to power, though his earliest biography, written in 642, suggests that it was not until the reign of T'ai-tsung that he came to have any close connection with the T'ang court.[21] As with most developments of the first half of the seventh century, the full implications of the connections established at this time only become apparent during the reign of the next emperor, Kao-tsung, under whom the religious policy of the dynasty changed slowly but steadily from the minimum positive involvement in religious affairs of the first two reigns towards something well on the way to a full-blown theocracy.

---

[20] *Chin-shih ts'ui-pien* (Shanghai, Sao-yeh shan-fang, 1919) 41:2b–3b (hereafter *CSTP*). Sun K'o-k'uan speculates on the role of Chi Hui in the study cited above in note three.

[21] Ch'en, *Tao-tsang yüan-liu k'ao*, pp. 47–50, collects all the early materials on Wang's life.

THE REIGN OF KAO-TSUNG (649–83)

Although the significance of Kao-tsung's reign for the development of relations between the Taoist church and the T'ang rulers is clear from even a cursory reading of the texts most scholars would tend to link the emperor's increasing involvement with Taoism to his ever more powerless position towards the end of his life. It might well be imagined that this unfortunate man, completely under the domination of the ruthless empress Wu and severely incapacitated by ill health, would have been glad to turn his thoughts to the unbounded freedom of the world of the immortals. Though the attraction of such an interpretation is undeniable it is also worth observing that Kao-tsung, whether through personal insecurity or political prudence, showed from the beginning of his reign an almost obsessive concern with the relationship between his family line and supernatural powers. There is at least a possibility that the developments of his reign in fact represent a deliberate attempt to reconcile the traditional symbolism of imperial rule accepted since the Han dynasty with the newer, more grandiose conceptions of the Taoist religion in a way that was designed to produce a powerful new brand of state ideology serving the needs of dynastic stability and continuity.

Thus at first glance the erection at imperial command of a monastery in 656 to commemorate T'ai-tsung would appear to be nothing out of the ordinary; T'ai-tsung himself had for example commanded the erection of the Hsi-hua kuan in 631, after Taoist prayers had restored the heir apparent to health, and the erection of another monastery, the T'ai-p'ing kuan, for Wang Yüan-chih. But the choice of name for this new edifice, Hao-t'ien kuan, was both unusual and significant.[22] For Hao-t'ien is no ordinary Taoist term but the name for the supreme power of heaven in the orthodox state cult over which

22 *THY* 50, p. 869.

the emperor presided. By this move early in his reign Kao-tsung was already taking one step which united symbolically the Taoist church, the state cult and the family line. Indeed, a pre-occupation with the relationship between the state cult of heaven and the rituals due to imperial ancestors may be traced back even further, to 651, when this was one of the main topics of concern in a court discussion about the Ming-t'ang, the ceremonial hall in which state observances were to be conducted. Subsequent discussions on this topic took place in 656, 659 and eventually 667, by which time the cult of heaven itself had undergone considerable modification; a recent examination of the terminology involved in the cult further suggests that these modifications made the state orthodoxy more compatible with Taoist conceptions of the celestial powers.[23]

At the same time the direct involvement of the imperial family with the Taoist church also became progressively more marked, though in such a way as to indicate a distinct reluctance to give one-sided support to the Taoists alone. Later in the same year that the Hao-t'ien kuan was built plans were set in motion to build a further monastery, the Tung-ming kuan, to mark the designation of the empress Wu's son as crown prince; the name indicates a celestial palace, "Eastern Light," at the opposite point of the compass from the palace of "Western Efflorescence," Hsi-hua, after which the earlier Hsi-hua kuan was presumably named. But though this monastery may have been intended by Kao-tsung to complement his father's foundation, it was simultaneously complemented also by the erection of a Buddhist monastery, the Hsi-ming ssu or "Monastery of Western Light." The derivative nature of this second name

---

[23] *TCTC* 199, p. 6275; 200, pp. 6297, 6316; 201, p. 6353; the terminology is reviewed in Fukunaga Mitsuji, "Kōten Jōtei to Tennō Taitei to Genshi Tenson," *Chūtetsubun gakkai hō* 2 (June, 1976), pp. 1–34.

suggests that this institution was an afterthought, even though in fact it was eventually constructed first.[24]

It is possible to suspect in this the hand of the empress. Though it would be hard to find at any stage of her career evidence of a positive antipathy towards Taoism her refusal to share the T'ang emperors' suspicion of Buddhism is well known, and the foundation of the Tung-ming kuan and Hsi-ming ssu is not the only example of support for Buddhism advancing *pari passu* with Taoism during Kao-tsung's reign. In 666, for example, after the performance of the *feng* and *shan* rituals of the state cult on Mount T'ai the emperor ordered the construction of three Taoist and three Buddhist monasteries in the vicinity; the distinctly non-Buddhist names of two of the latter once again suggest that some compromise had been effected. One establishment for each religion was simultaneously decreed to be set up in each prefecture of the empire, a move which did nothing to narrow the gap between the number of Buddhist and Taoist institutions, but clearly increased the proportionate difference to the advantage of the latter religion and gave it for the first time an empire-wide network of state-supported monasteries such as the Buddhists had already been provided with by the Sui dynasty.

In the same way an ostensibly even-handed policy was pursued in the court debates between the religions. Buddhist sources record five such debates between 658 and 668, culminating in a vigorous controversy over the *Hua-hu ching*, a Taoist text claiming that Lao-tzu had left China for India, where he had

---

[24] For details of these and the other measures mentioned below which affected both Buddhism and Taoism consult the chapter by S. Weinstein in the forthcoming volume of the *CHC*. There is some possibility, however, that the Buddho-Taoist conflict over the *Hua-hu ching* reviewed at this point has been mistakenly dated by our sources. See Wang Wei-ch'eng, "Lao-tzu hua-hu shuo k'ao-cheng," *Kuo-hsüeh chi-k'an* 4:2 (1934), pp. 147–268, especially pp. 216–17.

preached a diluted form of his doctrine adapted to the inferior spiritual state of his audience; this was the origin of Buddhism; the Buddha had been none other than a Chinese sage. Such a notion had already had a long history in Buddho-Taoist polemics and was to linger on for centuries yet. For though Kao-tsung obliged the Buddhists by ordering the destruction of all copies of the *Hua-hu ching*, this order was carried out in such an ineffectual way that copies of the text had reappeared openly by the end of the century. Yet it should not be imagined that this reign was dominated by a completely bi-partisan approach, as husband and wife advanced the interests of Taoism and Buddhism respectively. Examples of unilateral imperial support for Taoism alone, and especially for measures connected with the imperial family, are not lacking throughout the reign. One such project, an imperially-sponsored statue of Lao-tzu in 661, explicitly associates both emperor and empress with the imperial ancestor,[25] though it was not until 666, after the establishment of the nationwide system of monasteries, that a visit to Lao-tzu's birthplace led to his being honoured with a grandiose title, t'ai-shang hsüan-yüan huang-ti, which rivalled in splendour the appellations for him already current in the Taoist church.[26]

By this time important developments were also taking place in the fusion of the rituals of the Taoist church and of the state cult, in an area where Buddhists were unable to raise any objection. For Taoism shared with the common stock of native religious ideas a belief in the supernatural powers of China's mountains. The Buddhist monks who lodged on their slopes seem also to have accepted the existence of mountain divinities, but as latecomers to their domains were hardly in a position to control their worship. It was the duty of the emperor, on the other hand, to see to the cults of the mountain gods, and in 666

[25] *CSTP* 53:4b.
[26] *CTS* 5, p. 90; *TCTC* 201, p. 6347.

we find the earliest record of his use of a device for communicating with these gods which was particularly associated with the Taoist church and its pursuit of immortality. This was the metal dragon, to which written prayers were attached, and which acted as ballast when these were hurled from a precipice.[27] Various Taoist rituals were associated with this practice. Inscriptions survive indicating for instance that in 678 a ceremony termed a *ho-t'u ta-chiao* was conducted on Mount T'ai under imperial auspices by Yeh Fa-shan, perhaps the most famed magus of the T'ang epoch.

Yeh's biography in the *Chiu T'ang shu* states that he was descended from a long line of Taoist priests, and that he had come to Kao-tsung's attention as early as the 650s. He was to remain at court for the next half century and more, increasingly respected for his magical powers and political acumen and increasingly loaded with honours by a succession of rulers, until his death in 720 at the age of one hundred and six.[28] Though it is often unclear whether such wizards with a popular reputation for thaumaturgy who frequented the courts of the T'ang emperors were actually initiates of the organized traditions of the Taoist church or freelance masters of the occult, the titles given Yeh in the inscription of 678 and the nature of his duties at that time make it clear that he must be placed in the former category. Other church leaders do not seem to have achieved quite the same image in the public mind, but his long association with the court was not entirely unparalleled. Yin Wen-ts'ao, for instance, who suggested to Kao-tsung the construction of the Hao-t'ien kuan, had also accumulated a high court title by the time he died in 688. His services to Kao-tsung included not only the conduct of ceremonials, such as one at Loyang in 679

---

[27] The only full study on this practice remains E. Chavannes, "Le jet des dragons," *Mémoires concernant l'Asie Orientale* 3 (1919). This includes a review of the sources for the ceremony of 678 mentioned below.
[28] *CTS* 191, pp. 5107–8.

at which Lao-tzu is said to have appeared, but also the composition subsequent to this event of a biography of Lao-tzu, and other writings.[29]

These included what was evidently a polemical work, the *Ch'ü-huo lun*, a fragment of which survives in an encyclopaedia of the following century, giving Yin's annotations to a list of types of Taoist priest from the *San-tung tao-k'o*. This last work is known, from one integral text and quotations in the Taoist Canon and from a Tun-huang manuscript, under the longer title usually abbreviated to *Feng-tao k'o*, and is our main source of information concerning the ideal regulation of the life of the Taoist clergy and laity during this period. Various indications would place its composition in the mid-sixth century, but this quotation by Yin marks its earliest mention by another author, and perhaps indicates that an expansion of the Taoist church brought about by Kao-tsung's patronage had raised questions about the definition of the Taoist clergy. Intriguingly enough the portion of the work given with Yin's annotation, at least as preserved in our sources, ends without mentioning the *chi-chiu* or libationers, though other sources indicate that they were originally listed in the *Feng-tao k'o* itself.[30]

But perhaps Yin Wen-ts'ao's most important work, alas no longer surviving, was a complete catalogue of the seven thousand and three hundred fascicles of the Taoist Canon. This was apparently associated with a compilation of the canon in 675 in memory of the heir apparent, Li Hung, who had just died. Part of a preface to this compilation survives among the Tun-huang manuscripts, though by whom is unclear; both Kao-tsung and the empress Wu are known to have written prefaces, thanks to surviving references to the work of Wang Hsüan-ho, a Taoist who had these and other documents relating to imperial benev-

---

[29] *CSTP* 71:5a–6a represents our primary source of information on Yin.
[30] *Ch'u-hsüeh chi* (Peking, 1962) 23, p. 552. For the *Feng-tao k'o* see also the study cited in note 15 above.

olence towards Taoism engraved on stone in Ch'eng-tu in 683. Wang is known also through a concise encyclopaedia of Taoism included in the Taoist Canon, the *San-tung chu-nang*, which gives much useful information on such topics of current concern as rituals for dragon-hurling and the *Hua-hu ching*.[31] His collection of inscriptions in Ch'eng-tu consisted, besides the prefaces, of a copy of the edict conferring a new title on Lao-tzu in 666, of the edict establishing Taoist monasteries throughout the empire (presumably that of the same year) and of another document, dated 672, authorizing the ordination of the T'ai-p'ing princess.[32]

This last event demonstrates perhaps more clearly than any other the increased involvement of the imperial family with the Taoist church during Kao-tsung's reign. It was in fact the empress Wu who requested that her only daughter should be made a Taoist nun as an act of merit designed to bring repose to the soul of the child's grandmother, who died in 670; ironically enough, she had been a fervent Buddhist. This act may have been more symbolic than real, for we read in some sources that it was not until about 677, when the importunate Tibetans demanded a marriage alliance with the princess, that she was provided with a monastery, the T'ai-p'ing kuan, and installed as its abbess. The fact that a secondary monastery was later built for her which took the name of T'ai-p'ing kuan when she transferred to it suggests that this phase of her life was no temporary expedient, but by 681 the danger had evidently lifted and the young princess was able to demand and be granted a Chinese husband.[33] No less than twelve other princesses are recorded as

---

[31] *San-tung chu-nang* (in *Tao-tsang* 780–782, no. 1131) 2:8a–12a, 9:8b–12b.

[32] For these inscriptions by Wang and their connection with the compilation of the Taoist canon, see Yoshioka Yoshitoyo, *Dōkyō to Bukkyō* I (Tokyo, 1959), pp. 253–264.

[33] *HTS* 83, p. 3650; *TFYK* 50, pp. 870, 877.

having followed her precedent and entered Taoist communities
during the next two centuries, doubtless in many cases for
sound political reasons, but the life of the Taoist nun, devoted
to what had become the family cult of the imperial house,
might have represented a reasonable compromise between the
world of the palace and the shaven-headed rejection of all secular ties of a Buddhist nunnery.[34] To judge from the evidence of
literature the status of Taoist nuns was quite high, and they
were much admired for their simple yet striking dress, especially
their crowns and capes.[35]

Two years after the ordination of the princess, in 674, another
precedent was broken, though at first sight the connection with
Taoism is not obvious. For the assumption in this year of the title *t'ien-huang* by the emperor and *t'ien-hou* by the empress has
usually been explained as an effort at self-aggrandizement or
even a sheer flight of fancy, on the part of the latter.[36] But this
event was certainly prepared for through the circulation of
prophetic texts emanating from Taoist circles, and whereas
t'ien-hou, "heavenly empress," was a new term without any particularly striking resonances, *t'ien-huang* was quite the opposite.[37] According to the standard formulations of the received
ideas of the day as manifested in encyclopaedias and so forth the
t'ien-huang was first and most numinous of a series of primeval
rulers at the dawn of Chinese history. Early Taoist texts, such as
the *San-huang wen*, also speak of the *t'ien-huang*, but the connection with Taoism is usually dismissed in the case of Kao-tsung's
title on the grounds that subsequent developments in Taoist

[34] Sun, *Han-yüan tao-lun*, pp. 132–7; Benn, "Taoism as Ideology," pp.
344–5, note 24.
[35] See E. Schafer, "The Capeline Cantos: Verses on the Divine Loves of
Taoist Priestesses," *Asiatische Studien/Etudes Asiatiques* 32:1 (1978), pp. 5–
66.
[36] *TCTC* 202, p. 6372.
[37] For the prophecies see A. Forte, *Political Propaganda and Ideology in
China at the end of the Seventh Century* (Napoli, 1976), pp. 222, 224.

belief relegated the *t'ien-huang* to a position of relative unimportance in favour of newer, more exalted, divinities.

Quotations from both the sixth and the eighth centuries, however, show that whatever the opinion of some schools of Taoism a developed form of the *San-huang wen* circulated at this period which if anything stressed the importance of the *t'ien-huang* more than ever as representative of a long era of political peace and stability.[38] Even more significantly Buddhist polemicists of the early years of the T'ang had already put themselves on record as having no objection to belief in the *t'ien-huang* (they actually quote from encyclopaedias to illustrate the point), in sharp contrast to their total opposition to the higher Taoist divinities, whom they characterized with some justice as plagiarized versions of their own Buddhas and bodhisattvas.[39] When we note that the new titles were assumed in 674 on the Confucian grounds of filial piety to avoid any duplication with high-sounding titles bestowed simultaneously on earlier T'ang emperors and empresses we can only admire the adroitness with which Kao-tsung achieved the maximum amount of ideological value for the minimum amount of trouble.

From this time onward both the emperor and the empress seem to have devoted most of their attention to Taoism, and we hear very little of the activities of the Buddhists. Later in 674 the empress requested that the study of the *Tao-te ching* be encouraged; by 678 it had become a compulsory text in the examination system.[40] In 675 some further measures may also have been taken to promote the study of the *Chuang-tzu* also, but these did not lead anywhere,[41] though this year did see the

---

[38] See the full study by Ōfuchi Ninji in his *D ōkyōshi no kenkyū* (Okuyama, 1964), pp. 277–343, especially, pp. 325–6.

[39] Fukunaga, "Kōten Jōtei," pp. 1–2.

[40] *TCTC* 202, p. 6374; *THY* 75, p. 1373; *TFYK* 639:19a.

[41] R. des Rotours, *Le traité des fonctionnaires et le traité de l'armée* (Leiden, 1947), p. 386.

compilation of the canon mentioned above. 676 saw the emperor and empress journeying from Loyang, where the court was then residing, to worship the nearby mountain of Sung-shan, the Central Peak. Here they met P'an Shih-cheng, spiritual heir of Wang Yüan-chih, who had earlier moved to the mountain at his mentor's suggestion.[42] In 678 the relationship between the Taoist church and the imperial family may have been given institutional recognition with the transfer of administrative responsibility for the Taoists to the Court of Imperial Clan Affairs, Tsung-cheng ssu, though the documentary evidence for this is not as good as it might be.[43] The year 679 saw a second visit to Sung-shan and further discussion with P'an Shih-cheng. Despite his poor health the emperor seems to have felt unable to stay away from the mountain, ordering the conversion of a Taoist monastery there into a palace, the Feng-t'ien kung, after a further visit in 680, which also resulted in posthumous honours for Wang Yüan-chih. Though there is a certain amount of disagreement amongst our sources as to the sequence of events it is clear that the emperor then visited this palace on at least one occasion in 683, and that only his death at the end of that year prevented him from returning yet again to perform the *feng* sacrifices on the mountain.[44]

The present Taoist Canon contains a text named the *Tao-men ching-fa hsiang-ch'eng tz'u-hsü*, which is evidently a record of the discussions held between P'an Shih-cheng and the emperor and which reveals graphically the extent to which the latter's interest had by now turned towards the denizens of the Taoist heavens, perhaps in part because he felt that the time was approaching for

---

[42] Ch'en, *Tao-tsang yüan-liu k'ao*, pp. 50–2.
[43] Shigenoi, *Tōdai Bukkyō shiron*, pp. 144–5, and Sun, *Han-yüan tao-lun*, p. 78, both express doubts about this.
[44] Thus *TCTC* 203, p. 6415; Ch'en, *Tao-tsang yüan-liu k'ao*, p. 51 points to some contradictory references concerning the Feng-t'ien kung and concludes that there may have been two of them.

him to join their ranks. The first section of the work presents a concise summary of the origins and basic doctrines of P'an's religion; the last section is a little glossary of Taoist terms arranged in numerical groupings. But the whole of the middle of the work consists of answers to Kao-tsung's repeated questions concerning the population and organization of the unseen world.[45]

It is clear, however, that the emperor took seriously his role as intermediary between the worlds of men and of gods and was concerned that his own realm should be brought into concordance with that of his Sage ancestor. In the final month of his life the era-name was changed to Hung-tao, "Make Great the Tao," and it was decreed that no less than three Taoist monasteries should be set up in each superior prefecture, two in each middle prefecture and one in each inferior prefecture.[46] No doubt the inscriptions of Wang Hsüan-ho may also be connected with these measures.

One more measure remained necessary to conclude Kao-tsung's life's work: the proclamation of a posthumous title. This was of course the duty of his widow, but if it was a title produced simply on her own initiative without prior discussion with her late spouse we can only conclude that she had learned during the course of her marriage the art of reconciling family, state and church interests which Kao-tsung had shown in the naming of the Hao-t'ien kuan in memory of his father so many years before. For *t'ien-huang ta-ti,* as Kao-tsung now came to be called, was simultaneously not only a synonym for *hao-t'ien shang-ti* and (according to some texts) for his mortal name of *t'ien-huang,* but also, according to the *Tao-men ching-fa*

---

[45] *Tao-tsang* (Shanghai, 1924–6) 762, no. 1120 in the enumeration of the *Harvard-Yenching Index.*
[46] *TTCLC* 3, p. 15.

hsiang-ch'eng tz'u-hsü, a title for Lao-tzu in his divine aspect.[47] Kao-tsung's apotheosis may be seen in more ways than one as the crowning achievement of his career.

At this point it is necessary to consider the position of the empress. Having won the highest goal attainable by a woman of her time and place at the expense of the murder of her rivals she knew only too well that her own murder might well be the consequence of being supplanted by another woman, and had therefore bent her prodigious political talents towards making herself indispensable. The physical incapacity of her husband had fortuitously given her far more power than would normally have been the case, so his death (as she must have realised long before the event) left her in a highly anomalous position. To surrender her power would be tantamount to suicide; a dowager empress of such obvious talents as hers could not simply retire without becoming involved in the murderous court intrigues that would inevitably result. Yet to remain in power equally inevitably involved flouting the whole Confucian tradition of male rule. Nor could Buddhism, whatever her inclinations towards it, provide any obvious alternative ideological support for her; all the major objects of Buddhist worship were unquestionably male figures.

The one religious tradition in China that assigned any value to the female sex was Taoism. Not only had it absorbed cults of some antiquity devoted to the worship of such goddesses as Hsi-wang Mu, Queen Mother of the West; its most prominent school, the Shang-ch'ing tradition of Mao-shan, traced itself back to a female founder, Wei Hua-ts'un. In Taoist circles also the mother of Lao-tzu was no mere nonentity like the mother of Confucius but a "Mysterious and Marvellous Jade Woman," Hsüan-miao yü-nü, a being of supernatural dimensions as ex-

[47] For the first identification see Fukunaga, "Kōten Jōtei," p. 11; for the second Hsiao Chi, *Wu-hsing ta-i* 5, pp. 89–90 (TSCC), and for the third *Tao-men ching-fa hsiang-ch'eng tz'u hsü* 3:1b.

alted as those of her progeny.[48] The earliest document to indicate that the empress was interested in this aspect of Taoism
in fact contains references to both the mother of Lao-tzu and
Hsi-wang Mu, plus many other references to goddesses besides.
This is an inscription of 680 by Ts'ui Jung, the chief encomiast
employed by the empress, which was erected on Sung-shan on
the occasion of the imperial visit of that year. Its main purpose
was to commemorate the mother of the early Hsia ruler
Hsia-hou Ch'i, who had been metamorphosed into a large rock
on the mountain, but it is also a virtuoso demonstration of the
amount of female imagery available in the less Confucian
reaches of the Chinese tradition.[49]

Such imagery remained very much to the fore in the next few
years. Early in 683 imperially sponsored sacrifices on Sung-shan
were divided equally between male and female deities, the latter including both the mother of Ch'i and Hsi-wang Mu.[50]
Once Kao-tsung had died the goddesses gained even greater ascendancy; in mid-684 the Hsüan-nü or Mysterious Female, a
figure associated with the legendary Yellow Emperor, is said to
have appeared on a cloud of auspicious colour to confer an elixir
upon the empress.[51]   In the ninth month of the year the empress declared that the mother of Lao-tzu should not be left
without an honorific title after the T'ang had conferred a
lengthy one upon her son, and decreed that henceforward she
should be known as Hsien-t'ien t'ai-hou and that statues of her

---

[48] See Fukui Kōjun, "*Gemmyō naihen* ni tsuite," *Iwai hakase koki kinen
rombunshū* (Tokyo, 1963), pp. 561–7.
[49] See especially the copious commentary on this piece in Kao Pu-ying,
T'ang Sung wen chü-yao (Peking, 1963), pp. 1354–93; pp. 1358 and 1380
provide the main passages of interest.
[50] *CTS* 5, p. 110.
[51] Forte, *Political Propaganda*, p. 237; for the association with the Yellow
Emperor consult Kao, *T'ang Sung wen chü-yao*, pp. 1371–2.

should be placed in temples to Lao-tzu.[52] At some stage during the next half dozen years, if not earlier, prophecies in support of the empress deriving from the Lady Tzu-wei, an important goddess of the Mao-shan revelatory tradition, were also promulgated.[53] finally, in 688 the empress assumed the title of Sage Mother, Sovereign Divine, after the discovery of an omen foretelling the appearance of a Sage Mother (*sheng-mu*). This term had already been in use somewhat earlier to refer to the mother of Lao-tzu.[54]

There remained nonetheless one major disadvantage to the empress in the use of this aspect of the Taoist tradition. No matter what efforts she made to depict herself as representing a power yet more primordial than that of Lao-tzu, the great Sage Ancestor of the T'ang house, this only resulted in her becoming more closely linked with the Li family. When in 684 and particularly in 689 loyalty to that family became a watchword for dangerous rebellions against her rule the necessity of discovering some source of support unconnected with Taoism must have become increasingly apparent. Lao-tzu was accordingly stripped of his title in the latter year, though the empress, lacking any other sanction for her position, remained a Holy Mother and the *Tao-te ching* remained a set text in the examinations.[55] The following year, however, the Buddhists at length brought to her attention the *Ta-yün ching*, an erstwhile unimportant sutra which spoke briefly of female rule, and presented it to the throne together with a commentary designed to prove that it prophesied the ascendancy of the empress. Her title of Holy Mother was immediately dropped and she assumed open impe-

---

[52] *The Cambridge History of China* vol. 3, p. 292, mistakenly takes this to refer to the mother of the empress.
[53] Forte, *Political Propaganda*, p. 228.
[54] See Kusuyama Haruki, *Rōshi densetsu no kenkyū* (Tokyo, 1979), p. 346, note 8.
[55] *THY* 50, p. 856.

rial power on her own as first ruler of the new Chou dynasty.[56] For their help in this crucial move the Buddhists were soon rewarded by being granted precedence over the Taoists in 691, and two years later the empress substituted a text of her own devising for the *Tao-te ching* in the examination syllabus.[57]

It would be wrong to assume, however, that these moves led to any great rift with the Taoist establishment. Inscriptions on T'ai-shan reveal for instance that Taoist rituals continued to be performed at imperial behest throughout the Chou dynasty, and Ssu-ma Ch'eng-chen, P'an Shih-cheng's leading disciple, was apparently summoned to court at one point.[58] Even after the establishment of the Chou dynasty portents designed to confirm supernatural support for the empress continued to be reported in Taoist circles — an unfortunate embarrassment for the Li family which seems to have led to a certain amount of rewriting of the history of the period after the T'ang restoration.[59] But because the Buddhist church was plainly the recipient of much more lavish patronage, it is perhaps not entirely surprising to find one prominent Taoist cleric converting publicly to Buddhism in 696 and denouncing his former colleagues.[60] Similarly the one Taoist, Meng An-p'ai, who did succeed in attracting the patronage of the empress for the restoration in 699 of a phalanstery connected with her father, is

[56] The *Ta-yün ching* and the events surrounding its presentation to the throne are the subject of Forte's monograph, mentioned above.

[57] *CTS* 6, p. 121; *TCTC* 205, p. 6490.

[58] For T'ai-shan, see *CSTP* 53:4b–5a, and for Ssu-ma Ch'eng-chen, see Ch'en Kuo-fu, *Tao-tsang yüan-liu k'ao*, p. 53.

[59] For such portents see *WYYH* 561:1b–2a, 564:6b–7b. The former portent had been completely reinterpreted by 741 (see *TFYK* 53:18b–19a). Tu Kuang-t'ing, *Li-tai ch'ung-tao chi* (in *CTW* 933:5a–b), suggests that this reinterpretation and another besides were already incorporated in the official historical records of the reign.

[60] Forte, *Political Propaganda*, pp. 123–4, note 3.

also known through his one surviving treatise in the Taoist Canon as a thinker particularly influenced by Buddhism.[61]

It is also noteworthy that when the empress in her later years turned her thoughts increasingly towards the pursuit of immortality she seems to have been especially interested in Wang-tzu Chin, an immortal of no particular consequence in the pantheon of church Taoism. Rather, Chin's connections were with Sung-shan, which continued to loom large in her religious life. She appears to have performed the *feng* sacrifice contemplated by her late husband on the mountain as early as 688 and again in 696, and like her late husband built a residence there, which she visited in 700 and 701.[62] In 700 she received on Mount Sung a Taoist leader from Hung-chou whom she had commissioned to produce an elixir for her. This man, Hu Fa-ch'ao, headed a group so far removed from any established Taoist tradition that he appears in some of our sources described as a Buddhist.[63]

Yet this obsessive concern with Sung-shan may perhaps be explained by Chinese religious ideas prominent in Taoism. One source which gives details of empress Wu's special marks of favour towards the deities of the mountain also notes that later Hsüan-tsung paid special attention to Hua-shan on the grounds that one of the cyclical characters expressing the year of his birth

[61] See Ōfuchi Ninji, "The Formation of the Taoist Canon," note 5, pp. 255–6, in H. Welch and A. Seidel, eds., *Facets of Taoism* (New Haven and London, 1979), pp. 253–67.

[62] Forte, *Political Propaganda*, p. 235; Jao Tsung-i, "Ts'ung shih-k'e lun Wu-hou chih tsung-chiao hsin-yang," *CYYY* 45 (1974), pp. 397–412, especially p. 403. Cf. also Miyakawa Hisayuki on pp. 6–7 of "Tō no Genso to Dōkyō," *Tōkai Daigaku kiyō (bungaku-bu)* 30 (1978), pp. 1–13, which sketches some of the earlier religious history of the mountain.

[63] *TCTC* 206, p. 6546. Despite appearances to the contrary this can only refer to the same obscure religious reformer whose biography is touched upon in Akizuki Kan'ei, *Chūgoku kinsei Dōkyō no keisei* (Tokyo, 1978), pp. 109–10.

indicated that his destiny was governed by the divine ruler of the western sacred peak.[64] Kao-tsung's year of birth could certainly be construed as indicating that his destiny lay in the hands of the ruler of Sung-shan, the central sacred mountain. The year of birth of his empress is a matter of some controversy, but one recent study suggests that she may have been born in the same year as Kao-tsung.[65] Thus on the one hand her eventual public policy of curbing the prestige of the Taoist church serves only to underline the extent to which her late husband had already made it an instrument for enhancing the prestige of his own family line. On the other hand her own private concerns, especially in her old age, may well have been less with the compassionate Buddhas and bodhisattvas who received her outward worship than with the more sinister, purely native deities who formed part of the Taoist pantheon.

[64] *CTS* 23, pp. 891, 904.
[65] R. W. Guisso, *Wu Tse-t'ien and the Politics of Legitimation in T'ang China* (Bellingham, Washington, 1978), p. 210, note 50. For the authority of the ruler of Sung-shan over the cyclically indicated time concerned see e.g., *Wu-shang pi-yao* (*Tao-tsang* 768–79, no. 1130) 26:14a–b; this text is a compendium of the late sixth century.

The removal from power and eventual death of empress Wu in 705 had as little immediate effect on state policy towards Taoism as on any other area of government, but the restoration of the Li family did lead to one or two formal measures reversing the steps that the empress had taken to downgrade the importance of Lao-tzu and the *Tao-te ching*. The imperial ancestor was once again accorded the title *hsüan-yüan huang-ti* and his classic was reinstated among the prescribed texts of the examination system.[66] One positive step was taken besides to promote the interests of Taoism which was to set an important precedent for later imperial actions. This was the erection at I-chou in 708 of a stele bearing the text of the *Tao-te ching*. By promulgating the classic in the same way as Confucian and Buddhist scriptures, both of which had already been engraved on stone under earlier dynasties, the survival of the text for future ages was more reliably ensured.[67] But otherwise the return to the throne of Chung-tsung, a weak emperor much under the domination of his consort, the empress Wei, led if anything to increased imperial support for Buddhism. It is true that both Taoist and Buddhist monastic institutions were equally allotted state support at the rate of one establishment in each prefecture, but by deciding against the Taoists in renewed controversies over the *Hua-hu ching* the emperor showed a tendency towards

[66] *CTS* 7, pp. 136–7.

[67] See Chu Ch'ien-chih, *Lao-tzu chiao-shih* (Peking, 1963), who uses the text of this inscription as the basis for his edition, and *Chin-shih hsü-pien* (Sao-yeh shan-fang, 1919; hereafter *CSHP*) 6:6b–7a. Until the recent discovery of the Han text of the *Lao-tzu* this was widely regarded as the best available text of the classic, though it has been argued that the inscription appears to possess features peculiar to a recension widely used in the Taoist church but not actually faithful to the earliest tradition of the text; see Ch'en Wen-hua, "Lao-tzu 'Ching-lung pei pen' ti ch'ung-hsin k'ao-ch'a," *Tung-hai hsüeh-pao* 6:1 (1964), pp. 2–10.

partisanship where even the empress Wu had hesitated to favour their opponents.[68] Only the death of Chung-tsung in 710 and the subsequent downfall of the empress Wei brought about a change in the fortunes of the Taoists which restored them to the position they had held in the reign of Kao-tsung.

For whilst court politics remained for a time highly volatile all the main parties now involved manifested a degree of commitment to Taoism which suggests that Kao-tsung's dreams of a Taoist state had not perished during the intervening generation. Though Jui-tsung on his return to the throne proved hardly more forceful than the unfortunate Chung-tsung, he tended to defer to his sister, the T'ai-p'ing princess, who had, as mentioned above, passed some of her early years as a Taoist nun. Furthermore his son, the future emperor Hsüan-tsung, who had played an important part in ousting the empress Wei and her associates, clearly had an important stake in buttressing the prestige of the Li family, even if his personal commitment to Taoism at this stage was less than it later became. Hence in 711 the privileges accorded Buddhism by the empress Wu were further rescinded when Buddhist and Taoist clergy were decreed to have equal status on ceremonial occasions.[69] The same year also saw the return to court of Ssu-ma Ch'eng-chen, who had in the meantime been keeping clear of any political involvements by basing himself in the T'ien-t'ai mountains in Chekiang. But either a genuine desire to continue his eremitic way of life or a shrewd assessment of the as yet unstable state of the struggle for power led him to return south again, spurning

---

[68] For the details of this see the chapter by Stanley Weinstein in the forthcoming volume of the *CHC*.
[69] *CTS* 7, p. 157; *TTCLC* 113, p. 587.

even entreaties to move to the more accessible Mount Chung-nan.[70]

But the most spectacular result of Jui-tsung's patronage of Taoism was the increased foundation of Taoist monastic establishments, which in the main capital led to a more rapid expansion during his brief reign than in any other period of the dynasty. Jui-tsung himself ordered that the mansion of the empress Wei's son in the eastern capital should be turned over to the Taoists within months of assuming power in 710; one source suggests that he also handed over to them his own former residences in Loyang and T'ai-yüan.[71] Early in the following year he had a temple built for the worship of Lao-tzu and he is known to have supported a new construction project at one important provincial site as well.[72] In the main capital the residences of two daughters of Chung-tsung were converted to religious use, in one case after a son of the princess became a Taoist priest.[73] On top of all this the emperor then ordered that new and particularly sumptuous establishments should be provided for two of his own daughters, who were to be ordained Taoists nuns. The new titles Chin-hsien princess and Yü-chen princess were later selected for them to mark their new status, and their institutions were likewise named the Chin-hsien kuan and the Yü-chen kuan.[74]

[70] Ch'en Kuo-fu, *Tao-tsang yüan-liu k'ao*, p. 54; Paul W. Kroll, "Ssu-ma Ch'eng-chen in T'ang verse," *Bulletin of the Society for the Study of Chinese Religions* 6 (Fall, 1978), 16–30.

[71] *TFYK* 53:9a; *Li-tai ch'ung-tao chi*, in *CTW* 933: 5b–6a.

[72] *HTS* 5, p. 118; *CTW* 340:21a; and cf. pp. 135–6 of E. H. Schafer, "The Restoration of the shrine of Wei Hua-ts'un at Lin-ch'uan in the Eighth Century," *Journal of Oriental Studies* 15:2 (July, 1977), 124–37.

[73] *THY* 50, pp. 871, 876.

[74] *TCTC* 210, pp. 6659; for the exact sequence of events see Ts'en Chung-mien, *T'ung-chien Sui T'ang chi pi-shih chih-i* (Hong Kong, 1977), pp. 151–3. In *CHC* vol. 3, p. 341, these ladies are inadvertently designated sisters of Jui-tsung.

The eloquent protests of the large number of bureaucrats who were outraged by such reckless imperial extravagance are well represented in the official, Confucian sources for the period, which paint a graphic picture of the destitution inflicted on the common people through this misuse of the empire's resources of money and manpower.[75] Jui-tsung endured this barrage of criticism for more than one year until early in 712. Then, shortly before retiring from political life altogether, he agreed to halt the construction work, which must have been more or less complete in any case. This did not prevent him from complaining bitterly that "outside opinion" did not understand his intentions.[76] The ostensible reason for the extravagance had been that it served as a memorial to the late mother of the emperor, a truly pious and Confucian cause. The mother of Jui-tsung was, of course, the empress Wu, which suggests that the emperor's true intentions were to spend the surplus she had accumulated in the treasury in promoting the glory of the Li clan in such a way that it would prove less easy to supplant them a second time.

But neither Jui-tsung's retirement from politics nor the subsequent demise of the T'ai-p'ing princess at the hands of Hsüan-tsung served to interrupt the continuing process of the ordination of the Chin-hsien and Yü-chen princesses. For the various dates assigned to their ordination in standard historical sources represent not mistaken information but an accurate indication of the various stages that the process involved; a number of other sources confirm that this episode was no perfunctory gesture performed to satisfy an imperial whim, but a genuine and protracted religious initiation. Thus reliable epigraphic evidence suggests that the Chin-hsien princess, who was the elder of the two, had already received an initial ordination

---

[75] See the sources cited in *CHC* vol. 3, p. 341 note 26 (especially *THY* 50, pp. 871–5), and *CTS* 101, pp. 3136, 3158.
[76] *TTCLC* 108, p. 560.

in 706, though her sister seems not to have embarked upon the same course until after Jui-tsung had succeeded Chung-tsung.[77] For the ceremony which marked the "middle covenant" (*chung-meng*) level of ordination we are fortunate in having an eyewitness account by the Taoist priest Chang Wan-fu, preserved in his *Ch'uan-shou san-tung ching-chieh fa-lu lüeh-shuo*, a general work on ordination rituals. This event took place in the first month of 711, and seems to have been conspicuously extravagant. Chang is at pains to point out that Taoists do not care for riches in themselves, and is also forced to deal with the criticism that descriptions of such lavish rituals in Taoist texts refer to the world of the immortals which it is not for men to imitate in such luxury. His narrative in fact concludes by stating that in the tenth month of 712, when the sisters finally achieved the highest level of ordination, the ceremony was "a myriad times more splendid."[78]

Since Chang's work was composed two months after this last occasion his account gives a prominent place to the great Taoist hierarch Shih Ch'ung-hsüan, who presided over these events. Shih had risen from humble origins through his connections with the T'ai-p'ing princess and had become abbot of the institution where she had originally been destined to pass her days as a nun. But during this period, when the princess was playing an active role in the power struggles following the fall of the empress Wu, he accumulated an impressive array of court titles as well.[79] After the final ordination of the two princesses Chang became involved in another large-scale undertaking directed by Shih, this time the compilation of a catalogue of and phonological commentary on the entire Taoist canon. Though these

---

[77] *CSTP* 81:12b, and cf. commentary, p. 13b; *CSHP* 8:11b, the instructor of the younger princess is named here as Yeh Fa-shan.
[78] *Tao-tsang* 990, no. 1231, 2:16b–20b. *HTS* 83, p. 3656, seems to refer to an ordination in between those mentioned by Chang.
[79] *TCTC* 208, p. 6598; *TFYK* 53:9b.

works, which amounted to over one hundred fascicles, have not survived, a short summary of Taoist doctrine in one fascicle prepared at the same time, the *I-ch'ieh tao-ching yin-i miao-men yu-ch'i*, may be found intact in the present-day canon together with prefaces by Shih and Hsüan-tsung.[80] From the former preface it is possible to discern that the project involved not only Taoists like Chang but also many of the scholars who had participated in the production of government-sponsored compilations under the empress Wu. The work must have been completed by the seventh month of 713, when the T'ai-p'ing princess and her supporters were eliminated from the power struggle, since Shih was executed then, apparently to the general delight of the populace.[81]

The writings of both Chang and Shih suggest that by the early eighth century the Taoist establishment was no longer the exclusive preserve of aristocratic priests in the scholarly tradition of T'ao Hung-ching. Shih, in his restatement of the list of types of Taoist priest in the *Feng-tao k'o* already used by Yin Wen-ts'ao, draws particular attention to the *chi-chiu* and married Taoists, remarking that they concentrate on healing, are common in Szechwan and south of the Yangtze, and are qualified by their religious pursuits to be called *tao-shih* even if they have not abandoned lay life.[82] Chang, evidently a Taoist of the old school, complains bitterly in another work on selecting auspicious days for ordination that he has travelled in these areas and found Taoists there most remiss in their knowledge of ritual, and that now as a result of imperial support this sort of Taoism was becoming popular in the two capitals as well. He also complains about the adoption of the inferior rituals of the

---

[80] *Tao-tsang* 760, no. 1115. See also Yoshioka Yoshitoyo, *Dōkyō keiten shiron* (Tokyo, 1955), pp. 98–108.

[81] Chang Tsu, *Ch'ao-yeh ch'ien-tsai* 5 (Peking, 1979), p. 114.

[82] *Miao-men yu-ch'i*, preface 3a.

chi-chiu in rites for the dead.[83] The tensions reflected by Chang's most unecumenical diatribes may reflect changes brought about by the empress Wu, who in her dealings with Taoists, as with all her political actions, seems to have been prepared to extend her patronage beyond the circles which dominated the early T'ang.

But it was the very involvement of Buddhist and Taoist clerics in the machinations of court politics which formed for the young emperor Hsüan-tsung her most unwelcome legacy as he struggled to assert his power in the early years of his reign. After the fall of the T'ai-p'ing princess he acted firmly in 714 to curb the power of the clergy, and though these measures have usually been regarded as aimed at the more economically powerful Buddhist community they also included the Taoists within their scope in most instances.[84] It is not until the last great court Taoist of the preceding era, Yeh Fa-shan, finally died in 720 that we find Hsüan-tsung bestowing any favours on any Taoist, and even then the conferral of posthumous honours on Yeh can hardly be said to have overstepped the bounds of political prudence.[85] By this stage, however, Hsüan-tsung evidently felt that he had achieved secure enough control over the Taoist clergy to begin contemplating an active use of Taoism in promoting the prestige of the imperial house. To assist him he required the cooperation of a figure of comparable standing to Yeh Fa-shan, yet one who had emerged unsullied from the sordid political struggles of the early years of the century. Ssu-ma Ch'eng-chen, who all the while had been biding his

---

[83] *Tung-hsüan ling-pao tao-shih shou san-tung ching-chieh fa-lu tse-jih li* (*Tao-tsang* 990, no. 1230) 8a–b. Since Chang indicates that he is affiliated to a different institution from that to which he belonged in 712 this work probably dates form another stage in his career, so it is difficult to know which emperor is being indirectly criticized, though p. 1b indicates that he is writing fairly late in life.

[84] *CTW* 26:17b; *THY* 49, pp. 860–1; *TTCLC* 113, p. 588.

[85] *TFYK* 53:10a–b.

time in saintly (or astute) isolation in the T'ien-t'ai mountains, accepted the emperor's invitation to come to court once again in 721, and although he showed a continued reluctance to stay there, he helped the emperor to initiate changes in the state patronage of Taoism which were eventually to cause Hsüan-tsung's reign to be regarded by later ages as the high water mark of Taoist influence on Chinese political life.[86]

[86] Ch'en Kuo-fu, *Tao-tsang yüan-liu k'ao*, pp. 54–9. Ch'en conveniently assembles the considerable quantity of biographical material on Ssu-ma, which manifests occasional chronological contradictions.

TAOISM IN THE MID-K'AI-YÜAN PERIOD, 720–41

Although later historiography tended to regard Hsüan-tsung's involvement with Taoism as the senile preoccupation of his declining years, motivated perhaps by a mixture of megalomania and fear of death, such an interpretation must be at least modified in the light of the constant use of the Taoist religion by the T'ang dynasty prior to his reign. His later actions must also be acknowledged to be consistent with the policies pursued from 720 onwards, which far from showing an incipient fascination with the occult demonstrate a readiness to exploit the links between Taoism and the imperial institution over a broad front, albeit in a gradualist fashion. The nature of the emperor's contacts with Ssu-ma Ch'eng-chen in particular afford an excellent example of the wide range of Hsüan-tsung's Taoist interests at this time.

The patriarch was for instance among a number of Taoist priests and scholars who composed ritual music on Taoist themes at the imperial behest.[87] Although to describe the music of Hsüan-tsung's court would require a separate monograph in itself, it is enough to note here that these commissions had their precedents in Kao-tsung's reign, when P'an Shih-cheng had been asked to compose music, and that eventually the emperor himself also contributed to Taoist ritual music for use in the state supported Taoist cult.[88] Another precedent created by Kao-tsung was again taken up when Hsüan-tsung, after performing the *feng* sacrifices on T'ai-shan, turned his attention in 727 to the question of mountain cults. Ssu-ma Ch'eng-chen submitted that the ostensible divinities of the five holy mountains worshipped by the state hitherto were not in fact the true gods

---

[87] *HTS* 22, p. 476.
[88] *CTS* 192, p. 5126; Ch'en, *Tao-tsang yüan-liu k'ao*, pp. 297–99, collects most of the references to Taoist music during Hsüan-tsung's reign.

of those places; rather, ceremonies should be instituted in honour of the deities of the Shang-ch'ing pantheon under whose control these mountains actually lay. In response to this claim the patriarch was authorized to determine the necessary rituals in accordance with the Taoist scriptures, temples were decreed for each mountain, and Taoist domination of this important area of state ceremonial became complete.[89]

But the one event which marked most clearly the direction in which the emperor was to develop his support for Taoism during his reign seems to have occurred shortly after Ssu-ma Ch'eng-chen was summoned to court from the T'ien-t'ai mountains. In 721 the emperor ordered that the text of the *Tao-te ching* written by Ssu-ma in three calligraphic styles should be engraved on a pillar in a Taoist institution in the capital.[90] This move went beyond the earlier inscription of 708 in providing a text in triplicate, thus providing an exact parallel with the triple engraving of the Confucian classics on stone some five centuries earlier. The emperor's attention had already been directed towards the *Tao-te ching* in 719, when it had been brought into a controversy over the choice of commentaries for examination texts, in the course of which Liu Chih-chi (661–

[89] Ch'en, *Tao-tsang yüan-liu k'ao*, p. 56. *THY* 50, p. 879, would date this to 721, which seems too early, and *TFYK* 53:12a to 731, which seems too late even though it clearly refers to the implementation rather than the suggestion of the measure. *CTS* 192, p. 5128, in suggesting the date adopted here, coincides (as Ch'en shows) with an independent record of the establishment of a temple on Heng-shan.

[90] *TFYK* 53:10b. Ch'en, *Tao-tsang yüan-liu k'ao*, p. 56, prefers the date seemingly indicated in *CTS* 192, p. 5128, and Imaeda Jirō, on p. 24 of "Genso kōtei no *Rōshi* chūkai ni tsuite," *Chūgoku koten kenkyū* 23 (June, 1978), pp. 20–35, also appears to doubt the date 721, but it is not inconsistent with other developments.

721) criticized the Ho-shang kung commentary currently used in favour of the commentary of Wang Pi (226–249).[91]

It is noteworthy that at this date the *Tao-te ching* is discussed as but one amongst many classics, but from 720 onwards the text and its author were to be singled out for increasing attention to stand eventually at the head of a whole new branch of state-sponsored scholarship and ritual.

Thus in 730 we find imperially-sponsored lectures based on Lao-tzu's text taking place at court.[92] In 732 two more copies of the *Tao-te ching* were engraved on stone, together with an entirely new commentary under Hsüan-tsung's name, whilst in 733 the emperor ordered that a copy of the classic should be kept in every home, and that in the examinations questions on the Confucian *Shang-shu* and *Lun-yü* should be decreased to make way for questions on the *Tao-te ching*.[93] Next, in 735, an official sub-commentary was promulgated also, again under the emperor's name.[94] Then, again in 735, a priest named Ssu-ma Hsiu requested that the text with Hsüan-tsung's commentary should be engraved on stone at all places in the capital and else-where where Taoist rituals were performed on behalf of the state.[95] Honours such as these had never been accorded any text, Buddhist, Taoist or Confucian, at any time in the past.

The title given Ssu-ma Hsiu in the sources which mentions his request is *tao-men wei-i*. This indicates that during this period the Taoist church was being brought increasingly into the

---

[91] See William Hung, "A Bibliographical Controversy at the T'ang Court, AD 719," *HJAS* 20 (1957), pp. 74–134.

[92] *TFYK* 53:11a–12a.

[93] For these measures, and for the problems involved in dating them, see Imaeda, "*Rōshi* chūkai," and for one of the copies of the commentary on stone, *CSTP* 83:2b–6b.

[94] Imaeda Jirō, "Tō Genso gosei *Dōtoku shinkei so* ni tsuite," *Taishō Daigaku kenkyū kiyō* 64 (November, 1978), pp. 55–83.

[95] Ou-yang Hsiu, *Ou-yang wen chung kung wen chi* 139:13a (SPTK edn).

direct service of the dynasty as well. A funerary inscription for another important Taoist cleric named Chang T'an-hsüan, who died in 742, shows that the full form for Ssu-ma's title was *tao-men wei-i shih*, and that he and Chang both had this honour conferred on them in 733, though Chang's sphere of action was specifically confined to Loyang.[96] This full form, signifying "Commissioner of Ritual for the Taoists," is listed in Sung sources as one applied to prelates responsible for overall direction of the Taoist clergy on behalf of the T'ang dynasty.[97] That this was indeed the function of Chang and Ssu-ma at this time is confirmed by the biography of another Taoist named Liu Jo-shui, who was in 736 instructed by the *tao-men wei-i shih*, acting on behalf of the Yü-chen princess, to go to Mount Sung in order to collate Taoist texts.[98]

The institution of this office marked a radical break for the religious policy of the dynasty, since unlike some of its predecessors the T'ang had preferred to interpose no level of clerical representation between the civil authorities and individual monastic communities. Though scholars have recognized that in Buddhist circles this situation changed after Hsüan-tsung's reign, when government authority as a whole came to be exercised much more indirectly, the origins of the new policy in Hsüan-tsung's developing exploitation of Taoism have been quite overlooked.[99] Chang T'an-hsüan's biography notes that he had earlier been involved in the imperially-sponsored promotion of the cult of Lao-tzu in 726, but it may be that the post

---

[96] *CSHP* 8:9a.

[97] Kao Ch'eng, *Shih-wu chi-yüan chi-lei* (Taipei, 1969, facs. of 1447 edn) 7, p. 517.

[98] *CSHP* 8:6a; *CTW* 993:12a appears to place this event as early as 716, but an examination of the chronology of Liu's life shows this must be a mistake.

[99] For a summary of earlier scholarship, which relates exclusively to Buddhism, see Kenneth K.S. Ch'en, *The Chinese Transformation of Buddhism* (Princeton, 1973), pp. 116–124.

of *tao-men wei-i shih* was introduced as much to strengthen state control over the Taoist clergy as to promote their interests. Thus measures such as those concerning the registration of Buddhist and Taoist clergy introduced in 729, restriction on their movement in 731 and the enforcement of their obligation to reverence their parents (and thus admit symbolically their secular obligations) in 733 show that the emperor did not in the least intend that his sponsorship of religion should lead to any laxity amongst the religious community.[100]

Of course restrictive policies were aimed more at the Buddhists than the Taoists, since the former constituted the largest clerical group. The *T'ang liu-tien*, completed under the direction of Li Lin-fu in 739, gives figures of 3,245 monasteries and 2,113 nunneries for the Buddhists as against 1,137 and 550 respectively for the Taoists.[101] But the same source also notes that the clergy had in both cases an obligation to perform ceremonies for deceased members of the imperial family, whilst the Taoists were specifically enjoined to engage in ceremonies for the prosperity of the state both on the emperor's birthdays and on the *san-yüan* days.[102] The former occasions were instituted at the suggestion of Chang Yüeh in 729,[103] and the latter, which had for some time constituted the Taoist days of fasting in the middle of the first, seventh and tenth months, were marked out in 734 as days when all slaughter of animals was prohibited.[104] Concerning the days of fasting of the Buddhist calendar we hear nothing. The ceremonies to be performed are listed in the text; there were special ceremonies for the *san-yüan* days but otherwise the most common type was probably the *chin-lu chai*. Fragments of the rubrics for this type of ceremony have been

[100] *HTS* 48, p. 1252; *THY* 49, p. 861; *TTCLC* 113, p. 589.
[101] *TLT* 4:44b, 42a.
[102] *TLT* 4:47a–50a; *TFYK* 53:15b–16a.
[103] *CTW* 223:11a.
[104] *TTCLC* 113, p. 589.

recovered from Tun-huang, confirming that prayers were indeed offered up for the continual prosperity of the imperial line.[105]

Once Hsüan-tsung had addressed himself to the question of how the clergy should be organized to support the interests of the state various further modifications were introduced. In 737 the Taoist clergy were brought under the jurisdiction of the Court of Imperial Clan Affairs (Tsung-cheng ssu), to emphasize their connection with the imperial family.[106] In 738 it was ordered that Buddhist and Taoist religious institutions throughout the empire in suitably imposing places should be selected for state support and designated K'ai-yüan temples; in the following year it was further specified that these newly designated temples should be used for the emperor's birthday and the *san-yüan* festivals, whilst temples designated for state support earlier in the dynasty should be used for memorial services.[107]

But the emperor was soon to move on to more ambitious projects. The final year of the K'ai-yüan period, 741, belongs more properly in terms of its significance for T'ang Taoism to the succeeding T'ien-pao era, an era in which Hsüan-tsung's patronage of the religion was to produce cults and institutions entirely unprecedented in earlier reigns and which indeed witnessed an attempt to produce a Taoist form of government unique in Chinese history.

---

[105] Yoshioka Yoshitoyo, *Tonkō bunken bunrui mokuroku — Dōkyō no bu* (Tokyo, 1969), pp. 70, 80–1. Cf. Lagerwey, *Wu-shang pi-yao*, pp. 161–3.
[106] *THY* 49, p. 859.
[107] *THY* 50, p. 879.

TAOISM IN THE T'IEN-PAO ERA, 742–56

The total abandonment of the cautious religious policy of the earlier part of the dynasty that took place during the T'ien-pao period is quite apparent even from a cursory glance at the measures taken at this time towards the religious communities. In 741 a request that both Buddhist and Taoist clergy should in cases of criminal conduct be tried in accordance with regulations appropriate to them without interference from the civil authorities was granted,[108] but thereafter any attempt to pursue an equitable policy towards both religious communities seems to have been entirely relinquished. In the fifth month of 747, for example, the Celestial Master (*t'ien-shih*) Chang Tao-ling, the second-century founder of the movement whence most Taoist groups traced their descent, and T'ao Hung-ching (456–536), the great systematizer of Taoist doctrine, were granted posthumous titles.[109] In the first month of the same year an edict had authorized the ordination of Taoist priests as necessary to staff any Taoist religious establishments where numbers were lower than seven priests or where there were no priests at all.[110]

In neither case do we hear of similar measures being taken to appease the Buddhists, nor yet in the following year, when up to fifteen Taoists were ordered to be ordained for each place in the empire where a cave, palace or mountain indicated a site numinous enough to require an altar.[111] References to the copying out and distribution of ten copies of the entire Taoist canon in 749 and a further five copies in 751 similarly seems to

[108] *THY* 50, p. 865.
[109] *THY* 50, p. 881.
[110] *TFYK* 54:10b.
[111] *TFYK* 54:11a–b; *TTCLC* 9, p. 53. The mention of Chang Tao-ling and T'ao Hung-ching in this edict, if not simply a recapitulation of measures already taken, may indicate 748 as a preferable date for their ennoblement.

reflect entirely unilateral support for Taoism.[112] In this case moreover such support must be traced back initially to the K'ai-yüan period, when at some stage that cannot be dated precisely a definitive version of the canon was prepared on imperial command.[113] It would be misleading, however, to suggest that these signs of imperial favour were designed to promote the interests of the Taoist religious community as such. Rather, support for the Taoist church seems to have remained subordinate to the two major innovations of Hsüan-tsung's policy towards Taoism, both of which were designed to enhance the prestige of the imperial house.

The first of these was the organized worship of Lao-tzu, the imperial ancestor, which was designed to stress the supernatural origins of the imperial line and its continued support by supernatural powers. The second was the institution of a system of education and examination for entrance to the civil service based on Taoist rather than Confucian texts, which was presumably intended to introduce into the bureaucracy a group of men whose interests were more closely identified with those of the T'ang rulers than was sometimes the case for officials whose Confucian values might lead them into conflict with their sovereign. Both these innovations appear together in the late K'ai-yüan period, and throughout the T'ien-pao period both were subject to a process of continual modification which suggests that Hsüan-tsung considered them equally important.

Thus the earliest possible reliable mention of either a temple to the Emperor of the Mysterious Origin (i.e. Lao-tzu), a Hsüan-yüan huang-ti miao, or to a College of Taoist Studies, Ch'ung-hsüan hsüeh, occurs in an edict of 740, when the emperor decreed that a former residence of his in the capital should be converted for the joint use of two institutions under

---

112 *TTCLC* 9, p. 54; *TFYK* 54:16a.
113 See Yoshioka, *Dōkyō keiten shiron*, pp. 109–111.

these names.[114] This edict follows an account of a dream in which Lao-tzu had appeared to Hsüan-tsung,[115] and in the following year two more dreams of the same sort encouraged the emperor further in his projects: a large number of sources indeed associate his new foundations with these further manifestations of 741.[116] The first of these two dreams revealed the whereabouts of a statue of Lao-tzu, whilst the second resulted in the distribution of icons of Lao-tzu throughout the empire, a move which was followed in 744 by the further distribution of Taoist and Buddhist images together with images of Hsüan-tsung himself; the emperor seems to have been particularly interested in exploiting all opportunities for promoting his prestige through art.[117]

But the events of 741, and a yet more spectacular series of events in 742, were to have even greater consequences in the field of ritual. In the first month of the latter year, after a succession of miracles throughout the whole of 741,[118] T'ien Wen-hsiu, who was attached to the staff of one of the imperial princes, reported that Lao-tzu had appeared to him in the street and announced to him the location of a talisman, which the emperor then told him to retrieve. T'ien was naturally successful in this, and the appearance of this final portent persuaded Hsüan-tsung to

[114] *TFYK* 53:18a.

[115] *TFYK* 53:17a–18a.

[116] See J. J. L. Duyvendak, "The Dreams of the Emperor Hsüan-tsung," *India Antiqua* (Leiden, 1947), pp. 102–8. Fujiyoshi Masumi, on p. 827, note 4 of his "Kanri tōyō ni okeru Dōkyo to sono igi," *Shirin* 51:6 (November, 1968), pp. 795–829, favors 741 as the date of the founding of the Ch'ung-hsüan hsüeh; so too does Ting Huang, on p. 307, note 84 of his "T'ang-tai tao-chiao t'ai-ch'ing kung chih-tu k'ao," *Li-shih hsüeh-pao* (*Kuo-li Ch'eng-kung ta-hsüeh*) 6 (July, 1979), pp. 275–314.

[117] See E. Schafer, "The T'ang Imperial Icon," *Sinologica* 7:3 (1963), pp. 156–60; and "Notes on T'ang Culture III," *Monumenta Serica* 30 (1972–3), pp. 100–03.

[118] *TFYK* 53:19a–23b.

change the name of the era to T'ien-pao, Heavenly Treasure.[119] The talisman itself was placed in the new Hsüan-yüan huang-ti temple in the capital, which as a result of the innovations of 741 was now but one of a national network of such temples. In the ninth month this temple and its companions in the eastern capital and elsewhere received the more exalted title T'ai-shang hsüan-yüan huang-ti kung.[120] In 743 the titles were again changed: the temple in Ch'ang-an was named the T'ai-ch'ing kung, that in Loyang the T'ai-wei kung, and those in the provinces Tzu-chi kung.[121]

These changes in nomenclature were one concomitant of Hsüan-tsung's development of a system of rituals for the worship of Lao-tzu; another series of changes also took place in the titles applied to Lao-tzu himself. The measures of 743 formed part of a decree changing the sage's official appellation to Ta-sheng-tsu hsüan-yüan huang-ti, but in 749 this was further improved to Sheng-tsu ta-tao hsüan-yüan huang-ti in conjunction with a series of improvements in the titles of the emperor's more immediate ancestors.[122] finally in 754 it was decreed that Lao-tzu should be worshipped under the name Ta-sheng-tsu kao-shang ta-tao chin-ch'üeh hsüan-yüan t'ien-huang ta-ti, a title which identified Lao-tzu with the highest level of deity in the state cult of heaven and in the pantheon of the Taoist church.[123] The dominant role of the T'ai-ch'ing kung in the cult of Lao-tzu is shown by the fact that chief ministers were made commissioners of the temple, *t'ai-ch'ing kung shih*,[124] and by the constant modifications made in the rituals performed

[119] *TFYK* 54:1a–b; *THY* 50, p. 865; *TTCLC* 4, pp. 21–22.
[120] *TFYK* 54:4a; *THY* 50, p. 866.
[121] *TFYK* 54:5a–b; *TTCLC* 78, pp. 442–3. For the establishment, location and size of the first and second named, and also for the temple at Lao-tzu's birthplace, see Ting, "T'ai-ch'ing kung chih-tu k'ao."
[122] *TTCLC* 78, p. 445; *TFYK* 54:12b.
[123] *TFYK* 54:17b.
[124] R. des Rotours, *Traité des fonctionnaires et traité de l'armée* p. 14.

there; special provisions were already made in 742 prior to its renaming, and further steps were taken in 745, 749, 751 and 754.[125] Particular attention was also paid to the iconography of the T'ai-ch'ing kung; in 742 it was equipped with statues of the emperor and of Lao-tzu, in 746 statues of the emperor's chief ministers were added, and in 749 further statues of Confucius, Chuang-tzu, Lieh-tzu, Wen-tzu and Keng-sang-tzu were placed in the T'ai-ch'ing kung and (in this case at least) in the T'ai-wei kung.[126]

The T'ai-ch'ing kung seems to have been particularly favoured also by the unseen powers supporting the T'ang; appearances of Lao-tzu or other miracles are recorded as having taken place there in 745, 746 and 754, at which point the emperor ordered that these signs of special interest should be the occasion of a disbursement of gifts to the Taoist priests serving there.[127] Throughout this period a constant stream of miraculous happenings was reported to the throne from throughout the empire. In 749, as a result of the discovery of auspicious fungi (*yü-chih*) in this and the previous years and the discovery in the sixth month of the year of a jade talisman (*chen-fu*), Ch'ang-an, Loyang and ten other sites in the empire were ordered to establish Taoist institutions named Chen-fu yü-chih kuan.[128] It is by no means clear what special function these institutions were intended to fulfil, if any; they would seem to demonstrate an intermediate level of patronage between the sporadic foundation of single Taoist establishments, which was also continuing to take place, and the introduction of an empire-wide network of temples such as the K'ai-yüan temples and the temples to Lao-tzu. The last-named certainly formed the backbone of Hsüan-tsung's state-sponsored system of Taoist worship during

[125] *THY* 50: p. 866; *TFYK* 54:9a, 13b–14a, 15a, 17b.
[126] *THY* 50, p. 865; *CTS* 9, p. 220; *THY* 50, p. 881 and *TTCLC* 9, p. 54.
[127] *TFYK* 54:8a, 10a, 17a; *TCTC* 217, p. 6923.
[128] *TFYK* 54:12a, 13b; *TTCLC* 9, p. 54.

this period, not least because of their connection with his efforts to promote a distinctively Taoist system of education.

For according to the edict which established the temples in 741 they were to serve also as the premises for schools of Taoism in each prefecture, each staffed by one instructor in Taoist studies, the *ch'ung-hsüan po-shih*.[129] This did not provide an educational system as widespread as that of the Confucian schools, which existed also at the district level, but it represented a completely unprecedented extension of imperial efforts to increase the popularity of Taoism. These local "Colleges of Taoist Studies" (Ch'ung-hsüan hsüeh) bore the same name as the college in the capital. That college was certainly no anomaly when compared to the broad range of central academic and quasi-academic institutes already established in the T'ang period and when it is remembered that the Northern Chou and Sui dynasties had maintained Taoist institutions in the capital of an academic nature. But the simultaneous provision of a system of examinations, *tao-chü*, whereby an education in the Ch'ung-hsüan hsüeh could be used to qualify a candidate for entry into the civil service put it on a par with the highest educational institutions in the land.

As with the temples to Lao-tzu the years following 741 saw a number of measures taken to modify the provisions of the original edict. First experts in the *Tao-te ching, Chuang-tzu, Wen-tzu* and *Lieh-tzu* had to be found before in 742 posts for experts in these texts were instituted in Ch'ang-an and a student body of one hundred persons authorized.[130] In the same year the *Tao-te ching*, which had counted as a "small classic" in terms of length for the requirements of the regular examination system, was removed from this humiliating category so that it was only

---

[129] *TFYK* 53:18b; *CTS* 9, p. 213; *THY* 64, p. 1121. Fujiyoshi, "Dōkyo to sono igi," provides a comprehensive survey of Taoism in the examinations, on which the account given here is based.
[130] *HTS* 5, p. 142; *CTS* 9, p. 215.

examined in the *tao-chü*, though its study was of course by no means abandoned by candidates for other examinations.[131] In 743, at the same time as the change in nomenclature decreed for the T'ai-ch'ing kung and other temples, the Ch'ung-hsüan hsüeh in Ch'ang-an and Loyang were renamed Ch'ung-hsüan kuan and their *po-shih* were renamed *hsüeh-shih*, thus giving these institutions the status of academies and their teachers the status of academicians.[132] This emphasized their close connection with the emperor, but did not alter their function as teachers, though they were asked to perform additional duties such as public lectures on their texts.[133] The post of *ta hsüeh-shih*, or chief academician, was also created at this time, with overall responsibility for Taoism in the capitals; as with the *t'ai-ch'ing kung shih*, it was occupied by one of the chief ministers.[134]

The only significant change made after this date had more to do with Hsüan-tsung's continuing efforts to increase devotion to his sage ancestor than to further institutional refinements. In 754 the *Tao-te ching* was removed even from the examination curriculum of the *tao-chü* and replaced by the *I ching*.[135] That this indicated an increased rather than a diminished respect for the *Tao-te ching* may be gauged from the reasons for its earlier exclusion from the regular examinations and from a number of other moves during this period indicative of the high value placed upon it. Thus in 745 it was ordered that the *Tao-te ching* should be ranked as first of the classics, the most honoured

131 *TFYK* 54:3a–b.

132 *TFYK* 54:4b.

133 *TTCLC* 74, p. 443. This decree admits that the *hsüeh-shih*'s students were not yet very advanced in their studies, so they were given three years' grace during which educational testing was to be made less rigorous than normal.

134 *CSTP* 86:5b. *THY* 64, p. 1122, gives the name of the other holder of the post, who was promoted in 746 to the same rank (*TTCLC* 45, p. 223).

135 *TFYK* 640:4b.

position in all bibliographic listings and far superior to its normal classification amongst the works of the philosophical schools.[136] The same order decreed that the honorific title for Lao-tzu should be substituted for his name in all texts, and the whole measure (which also improved the position of the *Chuang-tzu* and other Taoist works) may be seen as an extension of an earlier move in 742 which placed Lao-tzu at the top of the received historical ranking of sages.[137] The further distribution of copies of Hsüan-tsung's commentary and subcommentary throughout the ten provinces of the empire in 755 shows that if anything increased attention was paid to the *Tao-te ching* after 754.[138]

The *tao-chü* examinations themselves were supposed to follow the precedent of the *ming-ching* examinations in their format, although one or two modifications were introduced.[139] On two occasions, however, special examinations on Taoist texts were also held to supplement the *tao-chü*. The first of these, an examination on the "Four Masters" of Taoist philosophy, was held by the emperor himself in the ninth month of 741.[140] The second was a decree examination named the *tung-hsiao hsüan-ching* examination which took place in 754.[141] The mention of "Four Masters" reveals an anomaly when compared with the list of Taoist masters (including Lao-tzu) honoured in the T'ai-ch'ing kung. In 741 we find no mention of Keng-sang-tzu. In the second month of the next year, however, the emperor asked for a discussion of appropriate titles for Chuang-tzu, Lieh-tzu, Wen-tzu, Keng-sang-tzu and the works under their names,[142] though a report of the fifth month of that

136 *THY* 50, p. 880.
137 *TFYK* 54:2a.
138 *TFYK* 54:18a; *CTS* 9, p. 230.
139 *THY* 77, p. 1404.
140 *TFYK* 53:22b–23a; *TTCLC* 106, p. 550.
141 *CTW* 522:4a.
142 *THY* 50, p. 880.

year reveals that no experts in the classic of Keng-sang-tzu had been found.[143]

The present text of the *Keng-sang-tzu* is well known to be the work of Wang Shih-yüan, who was active during the T'ien-pao period.[144] Since the report speaks of a need to make copies of the text in mid-742 it may be that Wang had realized the need created for a fifth Taoist classic to match the five classics of Confucianism and had already presented a copy of his freshly-composed work by this time; one early ninth century source even suggests that at first he tried to pass it off as a genuine ancient text transmitted through his family, and that when his forgery was detected the Keng-sang-tzu was not used in the examinations.[145] Why Wang should have attributed his work to a minor (and needless to say fictional) figure, mentioned in the pages of the *Chuang-tzu* and *Lieh-tzu* but hardly important, is a mystery, though the presence of Keng-sang-tzu in an inconspicuous place in the pantheon of the Taoist church may have enhanced his suitability.[146] What Wang was apparently forced to concede was that his "reconstruction" of the *Keng-sang-tzu* consists in fact of these portions of the *Chuang-tzu* and *Lieh-tzu*, padded out with other early passages drawn mainly from the *Lü-shih ch'un-ch'iu* and interspersed with thoughts on such matters as the recruitment of talent and filial piety which in all probability derive from Wang himself.

That the authorities in charge of Taoist education should even have contemplated examining students on such a melange of ideas, few of which relate to any form of Taoism, and that they should eventually have included the Confucian *I ching* amongst

[143] *THY* 77, p. 1404.

[144] Chang Hsin-ch'eng, *Wei-shu t'ung-k'ao* (Shanghai, 1957), pp. 856–60.

[145] Chao Chen-hsin, ed., *Feng-shih wen-chien chi* (Shanghai, 1958), pp. 2–3. Scarcely any questions from the *tao-chü* survive, but those that do at any rate make no mention of the *Keng-sang-tzu*.

[146] See Ishii Masako, *Dōkyōgaku no kenkyū* (Tokyo, 1980), p. 234.

their texts argues that the production of bureaucrats educated in an exclusively Taoist manner presented a number of problems. It is indeed rather hard to find among the many Taoists surrounding the emperor many who were simultaneously Taoists and bureaucrats. Some of the writings of Ssu-ma Ch'eng-chen such as his *Tso-wang lun* would seem to be addressed to a general audience including scholar-officials,[147] and references in Sung times to this work and to other writings by T'ang authors suggest that the Taoists of this period did in the long term achieve some success in creating a spiritualized "gentry Taoism" in competition with Buddhism.[148] But Ssu-ma's immediate impact on the ruling elite is not so clear, and the patriarch certainly shunned any administrative role himself. The same also holds true of his disciple Li Han-kuang, who succeeded to Ssu-ma's position of influence upon his master's death in 735; several of Li's writings (which have not survived) were devoted to the *I ching*, the *Tao-te ching* and the *Chuang-tzu*, which had been widely studied by scholars since the period of disunion as the "three Mysteries," *san-hsüan*.[149] In all Li was persuaded to visit the capital but three times, although the third time, in 748, he conferred a high level ordination upon the emperor. This was strictly speaking superfluous, since his master Ssu-ma Ch'eng-chen had already done this at his first appearance at Hsüan-tsung's court in 721, but the act

[147] For this work, see Tokiwa Daijō, *Shina ni okeru Bukkyō to Jukyō Dōkyō* (Tokyo, 1930), pp. 654–661.

[148] See p. 318 of Meng Wen-t'ung, "Tao-chiao shih so-t'an," *Chung-kuo che-hsüeh* 4 (1980), pp. 308–24; Wu Tseng, *Neng-kai-chai man-lu* 5 (Shanghai, 1960), p. 312; Yü Chia-hsi, *Ssu-k'u t'i-yao pien-cheng* (Peking, 1958), pp. 1213–14.

[149] For Li's biography and writings, see Ch'en, *Tao-tsang yüan-liu k'ao*, pp. 59–61, and E. H. Schafer, "Mao Shan in T'ang Times," *Society for the Study of Chinese Religions Monographs* no. 1, (1980), pp. 46–7.

was probably in both cases simply symbolic; there was a long tradition of honouring emperors in such ceremonies.[150]

The T'ien-pao period certainly saw an expansion in the number of Taoist priests charged with administrative duties. The only *tao-men wei-i* who is mentioned in sources of this period, and perhaps the sole occupant of the post, was Wang Hsü-chen. Wang may have been partly responsible for the compilation of the emperor's subcommentary to the *Tao-te ching* in 732, and by the time of his death in 755 he is described as having been "in charge of all Taoist priests."[151] But Wang was not without assistants; one, Hsiao Miao, is described as "commissioner for Taoists throughout the empire," *t'ien-hsia tao-men shih*, in one later collection of anecdotes,[152] though contemporary epigraphic evidence from 742 names him simply as a *chien-chiao tao-men wei-i* or "collateral Taoist ritualist."[153] This type of title implying a supernumerary appointment is attested in other inscriptions.[154] It is the subject too of an edict banning any further such appointments for Buddhists and Taoists in the capital on the grounds that they encouraged interreligious strife.[155] Since this edict implies the presence of Buddhist administrators also it is worth noting that Li Han-kuang already held during Hsüan-tsung's reign the title of *kung-te shih*, which was later used by the eunuch administrators of the Buddhist clergy, though apparently only on an *ad hoc* basis for one specific project.[156] The fact however that these Taoist administrative

[150] See Anna Seidel, "Le fils du Ciel et la Maître Celeste," *Transactions of the International Conference of Orientalists in Japan* 24 (1979), pp. 119–27.

[151] See Imaeda, "Dōtoku shinkei so," p. 82; *TFYK* 54:18a.

[152] Tu Kuang-t'ing, *Tao-chiao ling-yen chi* 1:3b (in *Tao-tsang* 325–6, no. 590).

[153] *CSTP* 86:1b.

[154] *CTW* 441:7a–10b, 990:21a–24a.

[155] *TTCLC* 113, p. 590.

[156] *CTW* 345:15a.

posts seem to have been equivalent to Buddhist posts which were never assigned to scholar-officials suggests that the occupants of these positions were not considered to be members of the regular bureaucracy.

Besides these priests turned administrators, the court of Hsüan-tsung was also frequented by a certain number of intellectuals who became Taoist priests. Foremost among these was the poet Wu Yün (?–778), chiefly known to posterity because of his friendship with his more famous contemporary Li Po (701–62).[157] Following a conventional education Wu had entered for the *chin-shih* examination without success, and had subsequently embarked on a wandering life that brought him into the company of a number of literary figures. After achieving a measure of fame as a poet he was summoned to court at the beginning of the T'ien-pao period, but left shortly thereafter to enter the priesthood. In 754 he presented the results of his Taoists studies to the throne in the form of a treatise entitled the *Hsüan-kang lun*, but otherwise seems to have preferred to continue to pursue his Taoist and literary interests in the region of the Yangtze rather than in Ch'ang-an. Wu's writings on Taoism may be compared to those of Ssu-ma Ch'eng-chen in that they seek to provide an intellectual alternative to Buddhism and would appear to be addressed to a general audience rather than to initiates, but Wu's standing as a priest was hardly comparable to Ssu-ma's, since he only received the initial *Cheng-i* ordination.

Yet Wu Yün's continuing use of his secular gifts as a writer in the service of Taoism after his entry into the priesthood was

---

[157] On the career and thought of Wu Yün, see E. H. Schafer, "Wu Yün's 'Cantos on Pacing the Void'," *HJAS* 41:2 (December, 1981), pp. 377–415; Kamitsuka Yoshiko, "Go In no shōgai to shisō," *Tōhō shūkyō* 54 (Nov., 1979), pp. 33–51; "Wu Yün's Theory of the Attainability of Immortality," *Transactions of the International Conference of Orientalists in Japan* 25 (1980), pp. 137–8.

somewhat unusual, since such a move was more often associated with retirement from public life. For example the scholar and official Ho Chih-chang closed a distinguished career in various academic posts in 743 by requesting imperial permission for his ordination and donating his own mansion to the Taoist church.[158] Yin Yin, a priest who in 737 was persuaded to embark on a career similar to that of Ho is particularly remarked on as having been allowed the special privilege of continuing to wear clerical dress, which again seems to indicate the exceptional nature of his dual role.[159] Hsüan-tsung's ambitious promotion of Taoism undoubtedly had a profound effect on his bureaucracy, and it is even possible to point to some officials who appear to have specialized in Taoist affairs.[160] But the Taoist priesthood and the imperial civil service remained essentially separate, and the ideology of the latter remained much as it always had done since before the advent of the T'ang; hardly as exclusively Confucian as the civil service of later dynasties, but ultimately based on an education in which Confucian learning preponderated over any form of Taoist studies. To change this situation was more than one man, however long and brilliant his reign, could achieve by himself.

Yet Hsüan-tsung's efforts to create an alternative to the traditional Confucian conception of monarchy were finally rejected only under later dynasties, and his many ideological innovations did not simply evaporate in 755 in the face of the rebellion of An Lu-shan. Rather the T'ang dynasty continued to draw on the reserve of ideological capital he had amassed until its final demise, and the fact that this process took a century and a half to complete bears witness to the efficacy of Hsüan-tsung's

[158] *HTS* 196, p. 5607; *THY* 50, p. 880.

[159] *THY* 63, p. 1101.

[160] E.g. Wei T'ao, for whom see *CTW* 307:11a–16a; *HTS* 122, pp. 4355–60; 196, p. 5606; *T'ang-wen shih-i* 50:17b; *T'ang-wen hsü shih-i* 3:5b–6a (rpt. Taipei, 1962).

strengthening through Taoism of the prestige of his family line. Even his arch-enemy An Lu-shan himself clearly assigned considerable importance to Hsüan-tsung's system of state support for Taoism; the chance survival of an inscription shows that in the territory which came temporarily under his control An took the trouble to rename at least one Taoist institution with his own reign title, Sheng-wu.[161]

[161] This inscription is listed on p. 118 of Fan T'eng-tuan, comp., "Kuan ts'ang Li T'ang mu chih mu," part 4, *Kuo-li Pei-p'ing t'u-shu-kuan kuan-k'an* 9:6 (Nov.-Dec. 1936), pp. 111–34.

Although Hsüan-tsung's successor Su-tsung (r. 756–62) was
beset during his brief reign with severe military problems in
coping with the rebellion, he did not neglect to take advantage
of the imperial connection with Taoism, though this connection was demonstrated through public portents rather than
through any institutional moves.[162] In 756 during his father's
exile in Szechwan favourable omens had already appeared at
Taoist ceremonies; the following year saw a theophany of
Lao-tzu himself, and in 759 a dragon was seen at a major noc-
turnal ceremony curled up on the imperial throne, where the
imprint of its scales and claws was duly shown to the morning
audience of officials the next day. Though no auspicious omens
are recorded for the intervening year it is recorded that Taoist
rituals were performed at the Department of State Affairs in
which the personnel of the department were obliged to take
part, and that a portrait of Lao-tzu was taken through the streets
of the capital from the Ta-ming Palace to the T'ai-ch'ing kung
in a particularly lavish procession. In 760 debates between
Buddhists and Taoists were started once more in a Taoist institution and to the accompaniment of Taoist rituals,[163] but after
this date Su-tsung's support for Taoism cannot be documented,
perhaps indicating that the Buddhist faith of his empress came
to have greater influence upon him[164]

---

[162] Cf. *THY* 49, p. 860; 50, p. 881, which would indicate that since 743 the
Taoist clergy had been under some sort of supervision from the *ssu-feng*, a
minor part of the Board of Civil Office, rather than the Court of
Imperial Clan Affairs, and that this was confirmed in 757. This period is
discussed by Shigenoi, *Tōdai Bukkyō shiron*, pp. 159–60.

[163] *TFYK* 54: 18a–b.

[164] For Su-tsung, his empress and Buddhism, see the chapter by Stanley
Weinstein in the forthcoming volume of the *CHC*.

All our sources are certainly agreed in depicting Su-tsung as an emperor much given to religious observances of every variety, and it would seem to be generally true that the more insecure rulers of the troubled latter half of the T'ang were far more prone to put their trust in holy men of all descriptions than their predecessors had been. In Su-tsung's case, as in many subsequent cases, the results were by no means entirely beneficial. A Taoist magus and confidant of the emperor named Shen T'ai-chih managed to accumulate a small fortune through his misappropriations in the Hunan area before Su-tsung was finally persuaded to believe the complaints brought against him by officials. It is perhaps no wonder that Shen's biography (a work of Sung date) in the Taoist Canon discreetly has Shen achieving immortality in 755.[165] Though such suspicious caution tends to confirm the account of Shen's career given in the biographies of his accusers the conflict of evidence clearly underlines the competing historiographic prejudices of our sources. An accurate historical assessment of Taoist personalities of the T'ang is yet more problematic than any account of Taoist institutions.

Su-tsung's successor Tai-tsung (r. 762–79) was without a doubt far more interested in Buddhism than in Taoism, though in some respects Taoism gained from his liberal policy on the ordination of clergy. Thus the regularization of previous irregular ordinations of Buddhist and Taoist clergy in the Honan and Hopei areas was granted in a pardon of 763, and in 773 and 774 measures were announced to increase the number of clergy at state-supported religious institutions.[166] But the Taoists seem to have been singularly unfortunate in that a plan to expand the number of state-supported Taoist institutions in 764 was

[165] For Shen's career as seen through the eyes of his bureaucrat enemies, see *HTS* 140, p. 4650; 145, pp. 4727–8; *CTW* 344:17b; for his Taoist biography, see *Yü-fu shan Shen Hsien-weng chuan* in *Tao-tsang* 201, no. 451.
[166] *TFYK* 54:19a–b.

turned down in the face of arguments against its extravagance, and when Tai-tsung did turn to the patronage of religious construction projects later in his reign it was the Buddhist who reaped the benefit.[167] His lukewarm patronage for Taoism may also be seen in that after the death of Li Han-kuang, the patriarch of Mao-shan Taoism, in 769 the warm relations that had existed between the imperial court and this religious center from the halcyon days of Hsüan-tsung's reign right through the troubled times following An Lu-shan's rebellion lapsed completely until much later in the ninth century.[168]

It is nonetheless possible to point to at least one Taoist leader who did receive strong support from Tai-tsung, namely the *tao-men wei-i* Shen Fu. In 772 two requests from Shen asking for the emperor to promote the performance of Taoist rituals were granted, and in 778 Shen was placed in charge of the construction of a Taoist monastery in the capital dedicated to the memory of Su-tsung.[169] Shen also assumed responsibility for the collection and recopying of Taoist literature from the provinces to make good the losses that had occurred during the rebellions.[170] Tai-tsung's support too for the system of Taoist education introduced by Hsüan-tsung, though faltering, was by no means absent. Though one of his circle of Buddhist chief ministers, Yang Wan, proposed in 763 that the Taoist examinations should be abolished, and though this suggestion seems to have been temporarily put into effect, in 768 he eventually decreed that the Ch'ung-hsüan kuan should maintain a quota of one hundred students.[171] finally, however Buddhist Tai-tsung's inclinations, he was still prepared to pick a title for his longest

[167] *CTS* 130, pp. 3618–20.
[168] See Schafer, "Mao Shan in T'ang Times," pp. 47–8.
[169] *TFYK* 54:19a–20a.
[170] Ch'en, *Tao-tsang yüan-liu k'ao*, pp. 125–6.
[171] *CTS* 119, p. 3431; *THY* 77, p. 1404; *TFYK* 54:19a. Taoist examinations were evidently in existence again by 776; see *THY* 75, p. 1373.

76

reign period that had strong Taoist associations: Ta-li (766–79) is a synonym for the *San-huang wen*, the same Taoist text investigated in 648.[172]

When the next emperor, Te-tsung (r. 779–805), acceded to the throne he put an immediate stop to the expenditure on Buddhist projects that had characterized Tai-tsung's reign and generally manifested an extreme reluctance to spend money on any form of religious patronage, though he apparently relented slightly in 787, when he ordered the construction of a Taoist monastery against the north wall of the Ta-ming Palace in Ch'ang-an.[173] But he did display an interest in the ritual of the T'ai-ch'ing kung and in the Taoist aspects of the examination system, in the latter case perhaps because one of his tutors had been a Taoist priest.[174] In 781 he altered the regulations for examining the students of the Ch'ung-hsüan kuan,[175] and in 785 both altered the ritual at the T'ai-ch'ing kung and introduced the *Tao-te ching* once more into the regular examination system. This latter measure was reversed in 796 when he concurred in the suggestion that it was after all not fitting to have such a sacred text included in the mundane context of the examination syllabus.[176]

172 See *Chen kao* 5:10b, in *Tao-tsang* 637–40, no. 1010.
173 *CTS* 12, p. 358.
174 *CTS* 190C, p. 5057.
175 *THY* 77, pp. 1404–5.
176 *THY* 50, p. 867; *THY* 75, p. 1374.

Hsien-tsung (r. 806–20), who succeeded Te-tsung after the brief and unhappy reign of Shun-tsung, seems to have continued his policy of maintaining support for Taoism whilst concentrating most of his energies on the important task of reasserting imperial control over areas which had become autonomous. When he was successful in this, indeed, the performance of Taoist rituals at the imperial behest constituted one way of marking the return of territory to the ruling house.[177] In 808 he is recorded as having sacrificed at the new year in person at the T'ai-ch'ing kung.[178] Though he is not known to have undertaken any new Taoist construction projects, he was prepared in 813 to expend a large amount of manpower and money on repairing the Hsing-t'ang kuan in the capital and providing direct access between it and the Ta-ming kung immediately to its north; the following year he increased its holdings of images, paintings and scriptures by transferring nine cartloads of such objects from within the palace itself.[179] This incidentally shows that the way in which imperial involvement in Taoism manifested itself in material terms was still very much after the extravagant fashion recommended by Chang Wan-fu.

In Hsien-tsung's later years he became increasingly involved with alchemists.[180] There is ample evidence that an interest in the alchemical pursuit of immortality was widespread amongst the elite of the early ninth century, but since Hsien-tsung

---

[177] See Wei Hsüan, *Liu Pin-k'o chia-hua lu* (*TSCC* edn.), p. 6.

[178] *TFYK* 54:20a.

[179] *TFYK* 54:20b.

[180] See J. Needham and Ho Ping-yü, "Elixir Poisoning in Mediaeval China," rpt. in *Clerks and Craftsmen in China and the West* (Cambridge, 1970), pp. 316–39. Hsien-tsung (and three of his successors) are discussed on pp. 317–19; pp. 323–5 translates another important source on alchemical fatalities from this period.

achieved a large measure of success in his restoration of T'ang power he may have been particularly tempted to find a means of halting not only the process of dynastic decline but also the onset of his own old age; to achieve the latter would clearly be of immense consequence to the former goal also. The only result of his endeavours, however, was that the chemicals he ingested altered his personality for the worse so that he finally had to be removed by a palace coup, or perhaps even succumbed to their deleterious effects without the assistance of an assassin.[181] But it is not clear that any Taoists were to blame for this unfortunate train of events. Liu Pi, the alchemist chiefly held responsible for Hsien-tsung's condition, was lodged for a while by imperial order at the Hsing-t'ang kuan,[182] but this may simply be an indication of that institution's importance to the emperor as the focus of his efforts to support Taoism at the capital, and may not mean that Liu was an ordained cleric — monasteries both Buddhist and Taoist served in the T'ang as lodging houses for gentlemen of any religious persuasion.

In fact, far from being a period when masters of the occult were allowed to spread their influence unchecked, the reign of Hsien-tsung witnessed the introduction of further refinements in the controls the government exercised over the clergy. In 807 both Buddhists and Taoists were put under the authority of the Commissioners for Merit, and any connection with the government departments that had been responsible for them hitherto ceased.[183]

It has been surmised that this measure followed the establishment in the previous year of an office to register the Taoist clergy, the *tao-lu ssu*, since a parallel Buddhist institution is known to date from that year, but there is no positive evidence

---

[181] See *The Cambridge History of China*, vol. 3, pp. 634–5 for the mystery surrounding Hsien-tsung's death.
[182] *TCTC* 240, p. 7754.
[183] *THY* 50, p. 881.

for this.[184] At all events these innovations did not lead to the abolition of the post of *tao-men wei-i shih*, which continued throughout the reign. In 810 one of the occupants of this post was a priest named Hsi I-su; it comes as no surprise to read that he was concurrently abbot of the Hsing-t'ang kuan.[185] Other sources record his presence at court debates between the three religions as early as 796.[186] By 815 we find another individual, Chao Ch'ang-ying, referred to as a *tao-men wei-i*; our source informs us that he was the disciple of Tai-tsung's *tao-men wei-i shih*, Shen Fu.[187] Chao's career extended at least to 825, when he is again mentioned, with the same title.[188] By this time, however, both Hsien-tsung and his son had met early deaths despite their pursuit of immortality, and Hsien-tsung's grandson Ching-tsung (r. 824–27) was on the throne.

For though the brief intervening reign of Mu-tsung started with the execution of Liu Pi and his cohorts, the new emperor's own demise, apparently the consequence of a polo accident, was probably hastened rather than retarded by the attentions of alchemists.[189] Once again, however, there is no indication of Taoist involvement in the production of elixirs for the emperor. Admittedly the year 822 saw the death of a thaumaturge named Wei Shan-fu, whose alchemical preparations had caused numerous casualties, and who was believed to have received a Taoist ordination (in the fifth century!), but he would appear

---

[184] See Kubo Noritada, *Dōkyōshi* (Tokyo, 1977), p. 247.

[185] *CTW* 495:8a–b.

[186] E.g., *Liu Pin-k'o chia-hua lu*, p. 13. These sources write his name Hsi Wei-su, but the correct form is confirmed by a poem addressed to him in *Ch'üan T'ang shih* (Peking, 1960) 276, p. 3135, which must date to before 805, the year of the death of its author.

[187] *CTW* 501:18b.

[188] *T'ang-wen shih-i* 50:17b. In 826 Chao is mentioned with a completely different title (*TFYK* 54:21b).

[189] *TCTC* 243, p. 7830.

not to have been summoned to court at any stage.[190] Mu-tsung's
only surviving edict concerning Taoism does at least indicate
that his attitude towards the Taoist clergy was entirely positive.
In the fifth month of 822 he decreed that anyone who wished
to enter their ranks and who could recite the *Tao-te ching* and
the *Tu-jen ching* from memory so as to show a clear familiarity
with them should be allowed ordination. Those who wished to
substitute the *Huang-t'ing ching* for the *Tu-jen ching* might do
so; applicants were to be tested by the end of the tenth month
of 822.[191] Nothing is said to indicate that a mastery of the ritual
or meditational use of these texts was to be tested; rather, a
reading knowledge comparable to that needed for the civil
service examinations seems to have been all that was required.

The time limit imposed on this scheme suggests that it oper-
ated only on this one occasion, but the texts named nevertheless
raise a number of questions. The *Tu-jen ching* as it existed under the T'ang was a small work in one fascicle that in a regular
Taoist ordination would have constituted but one of the texts
requisite for transmission of the Ling-pao scriptural tradition.[192]
It was not, however, simply read by adherents of that tradition.
An exemplar of seventh-century calligraphy has been preserved
which would appear to represent a summary of the text
designed to accompany pictorial representations of its contents,
a method of propagating the scriptures to a wide audience with
parallels in Buddhism. Since neither the calligrapher nor the
artist were clerics (they were in fact prominent officials of

---

[190] *T'ang kuo-shih pu* 2 (Peking, 1957), p. 46.
[191] *THY* 50, p. 867.
[192] For this work see Michel Strickmann, "The Longest Taoist Scripture,"
History of Religions 17:3–4 (Feb.-May, 1978), pp. 331–54, especially pp.
332–3 and the secondary studies referred to there.

T'ai-tsung's court) it may be presumed that the *Tu-jen ching* had a substantial lay readership.[193]

The *Huang-t'ing ching*, a treatise on the techniques of Taoist meditation, exists in two versions. The longer of these formed part of the Shang-ch'ing collection of scriptures, though neither amounts to more than a fascicle in length. It has been surmised that the Shang-ch'ing version was either a fuller text reserved for initiates, or alternatively that it was an expansion of the older, shorter version.[194] By the ninth century, however, there is plenty of evidence that even the longer version was widely read by persons with a very superficial knowledge of Taoism.[195] Earlier in the dynasty, as we have seen, the state was not prepared to recognize as ordained (for tax purposes at least) Taoist priests fully initiated in the more elementary scriptural traditions. Now the attempt to delimit the Taoist clergy within such narrow bounds seems to have been abandoned; rather, the state was prepared to confer ordination on individuals regardless of their standing in the eyes of the guardians of Taoist tradition. When this measure of Mu-tsung's is compared with the continued efforts taken by the T'ang into the ninth century to curb the irregular ordination of Buddhist monks the extraordinary nature of the emperor's decree becomes even more apparent. One possible explanation may be that by this period the interests of the Taoist clergy and the ruling house had become so closely identified that the political advantage of large-scale Taoist ordinations outweighed the loss of tax revenues.

---

[193] See pp. 32–42 of Naba Toshisada, "Tōdai ni okeru Dōkyō to minshū to no kankei ni tsuite," *Kōnan Daigaku bungakkai ronsō* 17 (1962), 1–42.
[194] See I Robinet, *Meditation Taoiste* (Paris, 1979), pp. 86–7.
[195] See *T'ai-p'ing kuang chi* (Peking, 1959) 46, pp. 287–8; 47, p. 295 (quoting the longer version); 62, p. 384 (quoting the longer version); 66, p. 408; 70, p. 437. The first, third and fifth passages here show that repeated recitation (hence also memorization) of the *Huang-t'ing ching* was a common practice.

By this time the *Huang-t'ing ching* may have been included amongst the works with which a candidate for the more testing imperial examinations was expected to be familiar. The handful of surviving questions set in the Taoist examinations, which date from 802 and 803, show only that the curriculum at this time must have been much the same as in Hsüan-tsung's day, in that no knowledge of religious Taoists texts is required.[196] But what is apparently an examination answer by Lü Po also survives which consists of a piece of rhymeprose elaborating on a quotation from the longer version of the *Huang-t'ing ching*.[197] All that is known of Lü is that he was once a candidate at the same time as Wang Ch'i (760–847), who passed his *chin-shih* examination in 798 and took further degree examinations in 803 and 808.[198] There is no conclusive evidence however to show that Lü's piece was written for any of these examinations, and the most that can be safely said of Lü's use of the *Huang-t'ing ching* is that it forms additional evidence that it, too, was widely read by laymen.

Despite the brevity of the succeeding reign of Ching-tsung, Taoist influence at court emerges much more clearly than in the case of his father. The emperor, a reckless teenager, showed an even greater passion for summoning holy men of doubtful character to his court than any of his predecessors, with the result that political leaders of both the main factions of the period were forced to warn him of his folly.[199] Although to judge from their remonstrances all the alchemists and magicians surrounding the emperor were charlatans of obscure origins, there is no doubt that at least some were regularly ordained Taoist priests of some learning. Thus Liu Ts'ung-cheng (763–830), though named in the standard historical sources as a Taoist

[196] *WYYH* 475:5a–6a, 476:5b–6a.
[197] *WYYH* 125:1a–2a.
[198] *WYYH* 133:5a–7a; *CTS* 164, p. 4278.
[199] *CTS* 174, pp. 4517–8; *CTW* 755:5a, 701:1b–2b.

priest of the Hsing-t'ang kuan, appears mainly as an evil presence inciting the emperor to search the empire for miracle workers and magic herbs in order to gain high titles for himself and money for his institution.[200] Yet a laudatory account of his career written at the time of his death reveals that he had been properly initiated in the Shang-ch'ing tradition and that he had spent some time in the religious life before his appearance at court.[201] Perhaps Sun Chun, another Taoist from the Hsing-t'ang kuan given a court appointment by the emperor, had similarly impeccable antecedents. Perhaps, though it seems most unlikely, even Chao Kuei-chen, a notorious figure who appears in our sources for the first time at this point, would have been shown to have had respectable religious credentials had his career ended peacefully in the same was as that of Liu.[202] To judge from the surviving evidence, however, Chao seems to have emerged suddenly from nowhere to receive the unprecedented title *liang-chieh tao-men tu-chiao shou po-shih*, Chief Teacher of Taoism for the Whole Capital, which sounds like an *ad hoc* post established because the post of *tao-men wei-i* happened to be filled at the time. Upon Ching-tsung's murder by his exasperated eunuchs Chao disappears from the sources as suddenly as he came, sent into exile in the far south.[203]

[200] *CTS* 17A, pp. 516, 520; *TFYK* 54:21a–b.
[201] *CTW* 62422b.
[202] *CTS* 17A, p. 519.
[203] *CTS* 17A, pp. 521, 523.

The reign of Ching-tsung's brother Wen-tsung (r. 827–40) was to mark a hiatus not only in the career of Chao Kuei-chen but also in the history of imperial support for Taoism as a whole. It is clear that Wen-tsung took seriously the T'ang policy of stressing the descent of the dynasty from Lao-tzu, since he ordered the repair of Lao-tzu's temple at Po-chou in 833.[204] He did receive one Taoist priestess from Mount Ma-ku in 837, and did grant special status to Mao-shan because of its Taoist community, but otherwise appears to have been extremely reluctant to extend his patronage towards any individual Taoist leader, or to devote much attention to religious questions at all.[205] But this marked no lasting change; the accession of a third son of Mu-tsung, Wu-tsung (r. 840–46), rapidly restored the *status quo ante* of two decades earlier. One of the first acts of the new emperor was to declare the birthday of Lao-tzu a three day national holiday, and within months Chao Kuei-chen had been summoned back to court and was bestowing a ritual ordination upon his new patron. There even appears to have been some scheme afoot at this stage to ordain all *ming-ching* and *chin-shih* graduates as Taoist priests.[206]

Wu-tsung's increasing preoccupation with Taoism emerges vividly from the diary of the Japanese monk Ennin (793–864),

204 *TFYK* 54:22a; *TTCLC* 113, p. 591.
205 *TFYK* 54:22a; Schafer, "Mao Shan in T'ang Times," p. 48.
206 For these measures, see *TFYK* 54:22a–b; *CTS* 18A, pp. 584–6; *THY* 50, p. 868. There would appear to be some confusion as to whether the measures described took place in 840 or 841. *TCTC* 246, p. 7952, provides a yet more confusing discussion of the sources which in reviewing the ordination of examination candidates flatly contradicts *THY*, though it would appear to be supported by some remarks made at a later date by Ennin in his diary. See Ono Katsutoshi, *Nittō guhō junrei kōki no kenkyū* (Tokyo, 1966), vol. 4, pp. 71, 87–88; Edwin O. Reischauer, *Ennin's Diary* (New York, 1955), pp. 347–8.

though he can hardly be termed a neutral witness. On the seventh day of the first month of 841 he notes that the emperor visited the T'ai-ch'ing kung (as his grandfather Hsien-tsung had also done at the new year); two days later he mentions public lectures on Buddhism.[207] On the eleventh day of the sixth month he reports that as a result of court debates between the religions to mark Wu-tsung's birthday two Taoist priests had been awarded purple robes while their Buddhist opponents had not; entries to the same effect may be found on the same date in 841 and 843.[208] In the third month of 844 he describes a ritual involving eighty-one Taoist priests at the imperial palace, and observes that Wu-tsung had already replaced Buddhist places of worship in the palace with Taoist ones. The Taoists, he says, had quoted an apocryphal prophecy of Confucius that the eighteenth ruler of the T'ang would be replaced by black-robed men; that is, by Buddhist monks, according to their interpretation. Hence increasingly severe measures were being taken against the Buddhists, even as the emperor was spending large sums of money on a Taoist nunnery and on the Hsing-t'ang kuan.[209] Though Taoist monks successful in rain-making ceremonies were being liberally rewarded, Ennin complains four months later, their Buddhist colleagues were receiving nothing.[210]

Under the ninth month of 844 Ennin mentions Chao Kuei-chen for the first time, as the author of a memorial requesting the construction of a "Terrace of the Immortals" (*hsien-t'ai*), as a means for the emperor himself to achieve immortality. By the next month construction was already under

[207] Reischauer, pp. 298–9; Ono, vol. 3, pp. 337, 340, 350. On the propagation of Taoism by public lecture, see also Michihata Ryōshū, "Dōkyō no zokkō ni tsuite," *Shina Bukkyō shigaku* 5:2 (August, 1941), pp. 23–31.
[208] Reischauer, pp. 308, 320, 330; Ono, vol. 3, pp. 399, 456, vol. 4, pp. 5–6.
[209] Reischauer, pp. 341–4; Ono, vol. 4, pp. 55–6.
[210] Reischauer, p. 348; Ono, vol. 4, p. 71.

way, spurred on by Wu-tsung's casual killing of one of the officials in charge of the work.[211] In the first month of 845 an edict ordering the manufacture of an elixir of immortality is referred to, and again Chao Kuei-chen is mentioned as involved in the project.[212] Ennin's next diary entry, exactly two months later, describes in some detail the extravagant decoration on the newly-completed Terrace of the Immortals, the emperor's increasingly obsessive behaviour and the discomfiture of Chao Kuei-chen and his supporters at their inability to provide their ruler with any results. Ennin attributes the initiative for the vigorous anti-Buddhist decrees promulgated at this time to the Taoists, who blamed their failures on the deleterious influence of the Buddhist religion.[213]

Though the subsequent pages of his diary are mainly taken up by his record of the personal difficulties in which he was involved by the nationwide persecution of Buddhism, under the twenty-seventh day of the eighth month he does note one or two of the more bizarre edicts issued by the emperor as a result of his by now totally irrational pursuit of immortality, such as a ban on wheelbarrows because they broke up the center of the road, a phrase that could also be construed to mean the "heart of Taoism" (*tao chung hsin*), and an order that the hearts and livers of fifteen year old boys and girls should be forwarded to the capital, presumably in order to provide materials for the elixir of immortality.[214] Mercifully for his subjects Wu-tsung died from alchemical poisoning in the third month of 846; this though evidence in the form of an inscription on a metal dragon which survived into the Sung shows that in the preceding year he had

[211] Reischauer, pp. 351–2; Ono, vol. 4, pp. 95, 103–4. On p. 106 Ono cites some precedents for the *hsien-t'ai* as a means of contacting immortals.
[212] Reischauer, pp. 354–5; Ono, vol. 4, p. 111.
[213] Reischauer, pp. 355–7; Ono, vol. 4, pp. 118–9.
[214] Reischauer, pp. 385–6; Ono, vol. 4, p. 234. For the belief that the organs of young persons were necessary for the preparation of the elixir of immortality, cf. *TCTC* 181, p. 5658.

confidently described himself as a *chen-jen*, a "realized man" or immortal.[215]

Though from the foregoing summary of Ennin's diary it might appear that Chao Kuei-chen and the emperor himself were the prime movers in the grotesquely tragic events in which the Japanese monk found himself involved, no account of this period would be complete without some attempt at assessing the part played by Wu-tsung's chief minister Li Te-yü (787-850). Li occupied a position of paramount influence at Wu-tsung's court, yet his attitude to Wu-tsung's involvement with Taoism was clearly not as straightforward as that of Chao Kuei-chen. During the reign of Ching-tsung Li had been one of the political figures who had (as mentioned above) cautioned the emperor of that time against reliance on men such as Chao. By 844 Wu-tsung had restored to Chao the very titles that he had held under Ching-tsung, and in 845 Li was so disturbed by Chao's influence over his sovereign as to be moved to bring up the matter of the Taoist priest's past meddling in court politics only to have the emperor shrug off his complaints in a most offhand fashion.[216] Yet Ennin reveals quite unambiguously that Li was partly responsible for an order in 844 reviving the national observance of the *san-yüan* days decreed by Hsüan-tsung in place of the Buddhist periods of fasting that had apparently been readopted in the meantime.[217] It is of course impossible to reduce the causes of the Hui-ch'ang persecution of Buddhism simply to personal animosities — a full consideration of the background of the persecution would go well beyond a description of interreligious rivalries to take in a general survey of the whole position of Buddhism in Chinese

[215] *TCTC* 248, p. 8024.

[216] *CTS* 18A, pp. 600, 603. *THY* 50, p. 868, puts Chao's restoration to his former status as early as 842.

[217] Reischauer, pp. 340–1; Ono, vol. 4, p. 55 and pp. 61–3 for an explanation of the background to this order.

society. But obviously the attitude of the main participants in the events of the period were not without their influence, even granted in Li's case that he was too astute a politician to be guided entirely by religious bias and that his treatment of Buddhism was probably influenced much more by reasons of state.

In fact there is plenty of evidence that Li Te-yü's personal inclinations were strongly in favour of Taoism. An inscription of 826 shows that he was already describing himself as a disciple of Taoism at that date, and careful research has revealed that his principal wife, one subsidiary wife, one daughter-in-law and one granddaughter all spent some time as Taoist nuns. [218] Li's relations with the Taoists of Mao-shan were particularly close, especially during the patriarchate of Sun Chih-ch'ing. It was probably because of his friendship with Li that Sun was commissioned by Wu-tsung to conduct Taoist ceremonies on Mao-shan in 841. [219] Perhaps only the death of Sun shortly thereafter and the rather unimpressive religious standing of his successor, who was ordained a priest not long before his master's death, prevented the summoning of a Mao-shan Taoist to court. Alternatively opposition from Chao Kuei-chen may have been responsible, since there may well have been a difference between the Taoism of Li Te-yü, an aristocrat who patronized a religious lineage that had been closely connected with the T'ang dynasty since the seventh century, and that of Chao, about whose background we know nothing. That the Taoist faith of his ancestors was important to the emperor is made clear by a prayer of his preserved in a later compilation of Taoist ritual in which (in the tenth month of 845) he draws the attention of the gods to the favours they bestowed on Kao-tsu and

[218] *CTW* 708:4b–5a; *Ou-yang Wen-chung kung wen-chi* 142:3a–b; Ch'en Yin-k'o, *Chin-ming-kuan ts'ung-kao erh pien* (Shanghai, 1980), pp. 37–45.
[219] Schafer, "Mao Shan in T'ang Times," pp. 48–9.

T'ai-tsung before begging them to come to his own aid.[220] But some hint that Chao was a religious parvenu to whom tradition meant little may perhaps be gleaned from the career of a contemporary Taoist master, Liu Hsüan-ching.

According to some sources Liu arrived in the capital at Wu-tsung's request as early as 841, and was responsible with Chao for urging the persecution of Buddhism.[221] Ennin, however, makes no mention of him, and it would seem much more likely that he made no appearance at court until late in 845, when he had so many honours and titles thrust upon him that he immediately begged permission to retire once more to his retreat on distant Heng-shan.[222] Since at this time an edict made him entirely responsible for all Taoist ordinations and initiations into the various scriptural traditions it seems quite possible that Chao, despite his impressive titles, was not considered to be of sufficiently advanced status as a master of Taoist arcana to be given this responsibility. Furthermore despite accounts in some sources of Liu's suffering the same fate as Chao Kuei-chen in 846, he evidently emerged from his entanglement in the politics of Wu-tsung's court unscathed and untarnished enough to confer a ceremonial ordination on the new emperor Hsiuan-tsung by the end of the same year.[223] This too suggests that the authorities drew a distinction between Liu, a man who had devoted a lifetime to religious training, and the opportunistic Chao.

It also suggests that Hsiuan-tsung (r. 846–59), even though he promptly rescinded Wu-tsung's measures persecuting

[220] *Wu-shang huang-lu ta-chai li-ch'eng i* 15:19b–21a, in *Tao-tsang* 278–90, no. 508.
[221] *CTS* 18A, pp. 587, 603.
[222] *TCTC* 248, p. 8020; *THY* 50, p. 869.
[223] *THY* 50, p. 869; *TCTC* 248, p. 8028. For the confusion over which Taoists were executed in 846, see Shen Ts'eng-chih, *Hai-jih-lou cha-ts'ung* (Shanghai, 1962), pp. 256–7.

Buddhism, was just as committed to the Taoist cause as his predecessor, and this is confirmed by a number of other events. In the first year of his reign he brought to completion the conversion of a Buddhist monastery in Loyang into a temple for the cult of Lao-tzu, a task that had been begun one year before. The installation there of representations of Hsüan-tsung and Su-tsung to accompany the icon of Lao-tzu himself indicates that Hsiuan-tsung was no different from Wu-tsung in emphasizing the by now considerable history of dynastic involvement with Taoism.[224] The following year the emperor bestowed a posthumous title on a *tao-men wei-i* named Ch'ieh Yüan-piao, though exactly when this man may have held office is obscure.[225] With the passage of time, however, Hsiuan-tsung's interest in Taoism began to shift towards the same reckless pursuit of immortality that had claimed the lives of so many of his clan. In 854 he ordered the repair of Wu-tsung's Terrace of Immortals, but was eventually persuaded to put the edifice to purely secular uses.[226] In 857, in the teeth of objections from his officials, he summoned back to court Hsüan-yüan Chi, a Taoist priest banished to the far south after the death of Wu-tsung as part of the purge of Chao Kuei-chen and his associates. Hsüan-yüan, however, had learned his lesson, and on arriving at court early the next year urged the emperor to devote himself to moral self-cultivation rather than alchemy. After a few months he was granted permission to return south once more.[227] But others (including at least one Taoist priest) were less scrupulous, with the inevitable result that by the sixth month of 859 the emperor

[224] *THY* 50, pp. 868–9.
[225] *THY* 50, p. 869. Ch'ieh may be no more than a miswriting of Hsi, in which case the name may be an alias for the Hsi I-su mentioned above.
[226] *THY* 50, p. 881.
[227] *THY* 50, p. 882; *CTS* 18B, pp. 640, 642; *TCTC* 249, p. 8065, 8067–8.

was ill and by the end of the eighth month he was dead and they had been executed.[228]

Since by now a fervent devotion to Taoism had conspicuously failed to save a succession of half a dozen emperors from an early death it is perhaps not surprising that Hsiuan-tsung's son I-tsung (r. 859–73) turned his patronage to Buddhism instead, and that we hear of no measures taken to support Taoism throughout the whole of his reign. Such indeed was his enthusiasm for Buddhism that he had to be reminded of the dynastic connection with Lao-tzu on one occasion in 861.[229] But this lack of interest in family tradition had no effect on the Taoist institutions that had already been in force for over a century. The Taoist examinations, for example, were apparently still being held regularly, although they had already been on a list of examinations needing reform in 856; one of I-tsung's more Confucian-minded officials complained about them again in 863, but to no effect whatsoever.[230] By the end of his reign, moreover, he seems to have been much more ready to greet any reported theophany or other portent with sonorous declarations of the divine antecedents of the T'ang line, for instance when attributing the final defeat of the rebel P'ang Hsün in 869 to the intervention of Lao-tzu.[231] The reasons for this are not far to seek, since it was during the latter half of the ninth century that the T'ang dynasty finally lost all control over events, so that its emperors eventually became mere pawns in the power games of the warlords vying with each other to succeed them. As military power slipped further and further from their grasp the emperors could do no better than rely on the waning ideological power of their position to assert as stridently as possible their divine right to rule.

[229] *THY* 48, p. 844.
[230] *CTS* 18B, p. 634; *CTW* 796:19a.
[231] *CTW* 933:12b–13b.

As a result of this increasingly desperate situation a considerable revival of imperial interest in Taoism appears to have taken place, particularly in the following reign of Hsi-tsung (r. 873–888), although to some extent this revival may loom rather larger in our sources than any preceding imperial campaigns to support Taoism simply because Hsi-tsung was fortunate enough to secure the services of a Taoist priest who was a gifted and prolific literary propagandist.[232] This man, Tu Kuang-t'ing (850–933), first came to Hsi-tsung's attention while the emperor was still in Ch'ang-an, but seems to have won his particular confidence after the court was forced to flee to Szechwan in late 880 by the rebel armies of Huang Ch'ao. apparently remained in the area even after the return of the court to Ch'ang-an in 885, for upon the final collapse of the T'ang in 907 he passed into the service of Wang Chien, an erstwhile petty crook who had established an independent regime in the Szechwan area that gave employment to many former T'ang officials.[233] During his long life Tu produced a large number of works on every aspect of Taoism from ritual to hagiography, many of which survive to this day, providing us with an unusually full record of the state of the religion at the end of the T'ang.

Amongst these the *Li-tai ch'ung-tao chi* is of particular value as a source for the Taoism of Hsi-tsung's reign, since it was composed in 884 for presentation to the emperor as a piece of pro-T'ang propaganda. Though it does provide some distinctly unreliable treatment of state support for Taoism prior to the

[232] For this revival see especially p. 33 of Li Pin-ch'eng, "Shih-lun T'ang-tai ti tao-chiao," *Shan-tung shih-yüan hsüeh-pao* 6 (1978), pp. 30–7. Also useful for a description of developments from the late T'ang into the Wu-tai period is Miyakawa Hisayuki, "Dōkyōshijō yori mitaru Godai," *Tōhō shūkyō* 42 (October, 1973), pp. 13–34.

[233] On Tu Kuang-t'ing see Imaeda Jirō, "To Kōtei shōkō," in *Yoshioka hakase kanreki kinen Dōkyō kenkyū ronshū* (Tokyo, 1977), pp. 523–32; and Yen I-p'ing, *Tao-chiao yen-chiu shih-liao* vol. 1 (Taipei, 1974), preface to *Hsien-chuan shih-i*.

T'ang, over five-sixths of the work is devoted to a highly laudatory account of the T'ang emperors, their devotion to the Taoist religion and the many conspicuous signs of divine favour bestowed upon them by Lao-tzu. For the earlier reigns it is possible, and indeed necessary, to check its assertions against other sources, but for the years immediately preceding its compilation our inability to corroborate all its statements is somewhat compensated for by the fact that Tu was probably a participant (albeit by no means an impartial one) in many of the events described. Thus under the third month of 883 we find a record of a report from Po-chou drawing attention to the many miracles whereby the T'ai-ch'ing kung there marking Lao-tzu's birthplace had been preserved from destruction despite the constant warfare in the area. In the eighth month this report duly elicited an edict directing that the temple should be renovated and that the parties responsible for raising the matter should be rewarded. Later the same month an auspicious inscription was discovered at the Ch'ing-yang ssu, a site connected with Lao-tzu's journey to the west, after the emperor had ordered that Taoist ceremonies should be performed there. Tu reproduces the congratulatory memorials that greeted this occurrence and the edicts rewarding both the discoverers and the Taoist institution that occupied the place. His final entry is the edict ordering the composition by a court official of an inscription commemorating the event.[234] This piece has survived independently, thus confirming the accuracy of Tu's picture of Hsi-tsung's preoccupation with Taoism.[235]

Curiously enough, Tu makes no mention of Wu Fa-t'ung, Sun Chih-ch'ing's successor at Mao-shan. According to sources connected with Mao-shan Wu is supposed to have conferred an

---

[234] The *Li-tai ch'ung-tao chi* is contained in *CTW* 933; Hsi-tsung's reign occupied pp. 14a–17b.

[235] *CTW* 814:6b–25a. For the legendary background to this event cf. Kusuyama Haruki, *Rōshi densetsu no kenkyū* (Tokyo, 1979), pp. 423–35.

ordination on Hsi-tsung by proxy in 882, but either this incident is a fiction or else Tu chose to ignore it for reasons of his own.[236] The latter probability is made more likely by the clear difference between Tu's catholic interest in all forms of Taoism and the narrower tradition of the Mao-shan patriarchs. Tu's teacher Ying I-chieh (810–94) was an heir to the same tradition as that of Mao-shan. Ying's teacher Feng Wei-liang had been a fellow-student with Wu-tsung's master Liu Hsüan-ching of T'ien Liang-i, who had himself studied under a disciple of the great Ssu-ma Ch'eng-chen. But Ying had also incorporated into his education a visit to Mount Lung-hu in Kiangsi, home at that time of the eighteenth generation head of the Chang family, the hereditary Celestial Masters (*t'ien-shih*) who traced their ancestry back to Chang Tao-ling in the Han dynasty.[237] References to the descendants of Chang Tao-ling are rare prior to Tu Kuang-t'ing, but because of Ying I-chieh he was well informed about the Changs and describes their exploits in his writings.[238] Thanks to the patronage of the Sung emperors the family was to become increasingly prominent from the early eleventh century onward, but there is no sign that the declining T'ang dynasty showed any interest in them, nor they in it.[239]

Tu also refers at several points in his writings to another Taoist tradition that had been steadily developing in provincial obscurity during the T'ang and that eventually rose to much greater prominence under the name Ching-ming chung-hsiao tao (The

[236] Schafer, "Mao Shan in T'ang Times," p. 49, does not make clear that his original source specifies an ordination by proxy. The emperor was trapped in Szechwan and was in no position to summon Wu to make the dangerous journey from Mao-shan himself.

[237] For Tu's teacher and his antecedents, see the *Tung-hsüan Ling-pao san-shih chi* in *Tao-tsang* 198, no. 444. This work, though misattributed, is actually by Tu.

[238] For example, in his *Tao-chiao ling-yen chi* 11:5b, 13:9b.

[239] For the rise to prominence of the Chang family, see Sun K'o-k'uan, *Yüan-tai tao-chiao ti fa-chan* (Taipei, 1968), pp. 18–33.

Pure and Bright Way of Loyalty and Filial Piety) during the Sung. This school had had brief contacts with the central court in the reign of empress Wu in the person of its reforming leader Hu Fa-ch'ao, mentioned above. There are also scattered references to it during the eighth century; for example, Shen T'ai-chih, the controversial magus of Su-tsung's reign, is said to have persuaded his emperor to erect a temple at one of its sacred sites.[240] Tu, however, gives a much fuller account of its hagiography, ritual and doctrine than any earlier source, and seems particularly exercised to explain its relationship to the established traditions of Taoism; he compares it specifically to the Ling-pao tradition.[241] Others at about this time appear to have been concerned to show its connections with the school of the Celestial Masters.[242] In reality the Way of Loyalty and Filial Piety had no historical links with established Taoism but represented a local cult in the Hung-chou area which grew in popularity to such an extent that the nationally established traditions of the religion were forced to take cognizance of it. P'ei Hsing, a contemporary of Tu Kuang-t'ing, testifies that its annual festivals attracted pilgrims from as far away as Szechwan.[243]

Though not many of P'ei's writings survive he shows an interest in Taoism almost as professional as Tu's. Little is known of his background; by 878 he held a fairly senior post in Szechwan, but he had earlier served in a junior position under Kao P'ien (ob. 887), perhaps the most capable general of the age. Kao, whose contacts with Taoists in Szechwan are reported by Tu Kuang-t'ing, was transferred thence in the same year to the lower Yangtze. In his new post Kao established a satrapy whose

[240] CTW 884:17a.
[241] In his Yung-ch'eng chi-hsien lu, p. 5, 16b, in Tao-tsang 560–1, no. 782.
[242] See p. 132 of the report by K. Schipper in Ecole Pratique des Hautes Etudes, V, Annuaire 88 (179–80), pp. 129–36.
[243] See Chou Leng-chia, ed., P'ei Hsing ch'uan-chi (Shanghai, 1980), p. 88.

allegiance to the T'ang court was more nominal than real, and his last years were marked by a conspicuous failure to fight on behalf of the dynasty and an interest in the occult rivalling that of Wu-tsung. He is said both to have received a Taoist ordination and to have constructed a "Tower for Welcoming Immortals" in his capital at Yang-chou. Other aspects of his religious observances, such as his worshipping the Jade Emperor (Yü-huang) have been seen as anticipating later imperial practice as it developed in five Dynasties and Sung times. Eventually Kao fell so much under the influence of his religious adviser Lü Yung-chih that his subordinates turned against him, imprisoned him and finally killed him. Prior to Kao's death Lü escaped and led his followers off to seek his fortune under another warlord, but he too was soon executed by his new employer. This bizarre episode serves to show that the attention devoted by P'ei and Tu to the Taoism of the provinces was no accident; there was ample opportunity by this stage to secure patronage from provincial power-holders only loosely connected with the central court, so that the more established traditions of Taoism which had won the support of the emperors earlier in the dynasty were no longer at any advantage.[244]

One such local notable was Ch'ien Liu (852–932), who by the end of his career had become ruler of his own kingdom of Wu-Yüeh and a most liberal supporter of both Taoism and Buddhism. In 899 he still performed the courtesy of asking permission of Hsi-tsung's successor Chao-tsung (r. 888–904) before undertaking the renovation of one famous Taoist monastery in his territory. The emperor was glad to give his blessing, since his own ability to see to the maintenance of the

---

[244] For a full account of Kao P'ien's career in relation to Taoism, see Miyakawa Hisayuki, "Legate Kao P'ien and a Taoist Magician Lü Yung-chih in the Time of Huang Ch'ao's Rebellion," *Acta Asiatica* 27 (1974), pp. 74–99.

Taoist establishment was severely limited.[245] He was in fact kept a virtual prisoner in his own court by the warlord Chu Wen. Survival was therefore for him a far more immediate problem than questions of religious policy, and it is perhaps not surprising that we hear nothing more of his attitude to Taoism than is contained in his brief reply to Ch'ien. Such responsibility as he cared to exercise for maintaining the Taoist institutions set up by Hsüan-tsung lay entirely in the hands of Chu Wen, not those of the emperor. In 903 Chu held a post that gave him nominal charge of repairing a T'ai-ch'ing kung.[246] Though the location is not specified, the T'ai-ch'ing kung at Po-chou would appear to be indicated, which would suggest that little had been done to the site since the reign of Hsi-tsung. Certainly it seems most unlikely that Chu Wen bothered to do anything about the matter.

In early 904 Chu moved the court to Loyang, and in the eighth month had Chao-tsung murdered in order to replace him with his twelve-year old son. The transfer to Loyang necessitated the designation of a T'ai-ch'ing kung in the new capital, a problem to which various solutions were propounded in 905. But though Chu allowed Taoist ceremonies to be conducted in the same year to counteract celestial portents of disaster, by 907 he had no further use for the T'ang dynasty and so dispensed with it and set up his own state of Liang.[247] The T'ai-ch'ing kung was promptly demoted to the same status as any other religious edifice and ultimate bureaucratic responsibility for the Taoist priesthood was formally separated from any connection with the imperial clan.[248] That these precautions were not entirely otiose

---

[245] For Ch'en Liu's religious policy see Abe Chōichi, *Chūgoku zenshūshi no kenkyū* (Tokyo, 1963), pp. 102–34, and for the particular incident in question p. 114 and *CTW* 91:18a–b.

[246] *CTS* 20A, p. 776.

[247] *CTS* 20B, pp. 792–4, 796.

[248] *TFYK* 194:19a.

may be inferred from an incident which took place at about this time under Wang Chien's rule in Szechwan, where a Taoist priest related to the T'ang line was involved in an abortive coup, presumably designed to restore the dynasty.[249]

This was not quite the end of the story, since in 923 Chu's Liang dynasty was itself snuffed out by the Sha-t'o Turks. Because their ruling family in the late ninth century had been adopted into the T'ang imperial house these Turks considered themselves true heirs of the T'ang and set up their own Later T'ang dynasty. As descendants of Lao-tzu by adoption they apparently felt that they should manifest conspicuous support for Taoism, so between 927 and 929 Chu's policies were completely reversed and T'ang observances such as the celebration of Lao-tzu's birthday introduced by Wu-tsung were revived once more.[250] The respite this provided for the crumbling institutions for the state support of Taoism devised by the early T'ang emperors was brief indeed, since the Later T'ang dynasty itself only lasted until 936. Thus the story of T'ang Taoism starts with a Turkish chief worshipping Lao-tzu ahead of the first emperor of the dynasty and ends with a Turkish emperor worshipping Lao-tzu in the place of that emperor's last descendant. Since the T'ang rulers were probably genealogically as closely connected with their Turkish neighbours as they were with any ancient Chinese sage the irony is perhaps apt.

But this was in one sense not yet the end of the story. For when the Sung dynasty was finally able to bring to a close the political fragmentation of the tenth century they too clearly felt obliged to pay particular attention to the cult of Lao-tzu, and were further put to the trouble of having to find an immortal ancestor from whom to trace the descent of their own ruling

[249] Sun Kuang-hsien, *Pei-meng so-yen* 12 (Peking, 1981), pp. 93–4.
[250] *TFYK* 54:23b–24b.

house.[251] Emperors of the succeeding Yüan and Ming dynasties also showed a considerable interest in Taoism and the relative indifference of the Ch'ing dynasty to the religion appears to have been the exception rather than the rule. Perhaps it is only because the Ch'ing was the sole dynasty with which Westerners had a chance to become familiar that we have until now accepted the picture of Taoists at court as due to the weakness of one or two aberrant emperors. The foregoing essay should at least give the lie to the Confucian version of T'ang history; the task of setting the events described in their larger context of religious development beyond the confines of the imperial court must remain a problem for future research.

[251] Sun K'o-k'uan, *Sung Yüan tao-chiao chih fa-chan* (Taichung, 1965), pp. 80–5.

Glossary / Index

103